More Advance Praise for
If This Be Treason: Translation and Its Dyscontents

"We owe to Gregory Rabassa the rediscovery of Latin America—through its literature. It is no secret that his English-language renditions of twentieth-century classics are, at times, superior to the original. He is a master whose lesson is humbling: Serendipity and intuition, and not method, rule translation. *If This Be Treason* is a jewel of a memoir that makes us recognize, yet again, the extent to which the translator is the closest one gets to 'a perfect reader.' "
—Ilan Stavans, author of *On Borrowed Words*

"Gregory Rabassa's witty reflection on his lifelong passion for translation, in all its (and his) ambivalent being, is as sparkling as his own work. Widely known as 'the translator's translator,' he brings his worldwide knowledge together with his renowned humor in considerations general and specific, on his extensive experience first as cryptographer and then as the finder of 'evergreen' words in the new reading that translation is."
—Mary Ann Caws

"Gregory Rabassa's enchanting new memoir, while engaging and humorous, also reveals the essential role of translation in our world today. Rabassa, the superb translator of Gabriel García Márquez and Julio Cortázar, recounts an adventurous life whose greatest adventure is an awakening to language. Through it all, his loyalty is to the word, 'the metaphor for all the things we see, feel, and imagine.' Bravo, Rabassa!"　　　—Grace Schulman

IF THIS BE TREASON

TRANSLATION AND ITS DYSCONTENTS

GREGORY RABASSA

IF THIS BE
TREASON

TRANSLATION AND ITS
DYSCONTENTS

A MEMOIR

A NEW DIRECTIONS BOOK

Manufactured in the United States of America
First published clothbound by New Directions in 2005
Published simultaneously in Canada by Penguin Books Canada Limited
New Directions Books are printed on acid-free paper.
Design by Semadar Megged

Library of Congress Cataloging-in-Publication Data

Rabassa, Gregory.
If this be treason : translation and its dyscontents : a memoir / Gregory Rabassa.
   p. cm.
ISBN 0-8112-1619-5 (alk. paper)
1. Translating and interpreting. I. Title.
P306.R33 2005
418'.02—dc22   2004028179

New Directions Books are published for James Laughlin
by New Directions Publishing Corporation,
80 Eighth Avenue, New York 10011

FOR MY DARLING CLEMENTINE

Summa mihi gloria

Traduttore, traditore
—Italian cliché

If this be treason, make the most of it.
—Patrick Henry

Contents

CONTENTS

If This Be Treason

Translation and Its Dyscontents

PART ONE

THE ONSET OF PERFIDY

I

THE MANY FACES OF TREASON

COMMONPLACES MAY COME AND GO, but one that has held forth over the years to the dismay and discouragement of translators is the Italian punning canard *traduttore, traditore* (translator, traitor), leading one to believe that the translator, worse than an unfortunate bungler, is a treacherous knave. Before copping a plea and offering a *nolo contendere*, let me see wherein this treason lies and against whom. Then we translators can withdraw once more into that limbo of silent servitors, for, as Prince Segismundo says at the end of Calderón's *Life Is a Dream* when he awards his liberator the tower where he had been imprisoned, "The treason done, the traitor is no longer needed."

Let us submit the practice of translation to a judicial enquiry into its various ways and means and in this display seek out the many varieties of betrayal which might be inherent to its art. I say art and not craft because you can teach a craft but you cannot teach an art. You can teach Picasso how to mix his paints but you cannot teach him how to paint his demoiselles. There are many spots where translation can be accused of treason, all inevitably interconnected in such diverse ways that an overall view is needed to reveal the many facets of the treason the Italians purport to see.

The most elemental of these will be betrayal of the word, for the word is the very essence of language, the metaphor for all the things we see, feel, and imagine. Out of this we also have a betrayal of language, in both directions (I try to avoid the jargon of "target language"; I am an old infantryman, and we dogfaces were taught to shoot at a target and, ideally, kill it). Languages are the products of a culture, or perhaps the reverse as some bold anthropologist might have it. Treason against a culture will therefore be automatic as we betray its words and speech as well as assorted other little items along the way.

Then we come to personal betrayals, those against the people involved in the act of translation. The first victim is, of course, the author we are translating. Can we ever make a different-colored clone of what he (read he/she, as in a U.N. document) has done? Can we ever feel what the author felt as he wrote the words we are transforming? As we betray the author we are automatically betraying our variegated readership and at the same time we are passing on whatever bit of betrayal the author himself may have foisted on them in the original (unless we have left it out on some Frosty morning along with the poetry). Lastly and most subtly we betray ourselves. We will sacrifice our best hunches in favor of some pedestrian norm in fear of betraying the task we were set to do. The facelessness imposed on the translator, so often thought of as an ideal, can only mean incarceration in Segismundo's tower in the end. This last betrayal must stand before all the treasons here delineated as the most foul.

Words are treacherous things, much moreso than any translator could ever be. As is obvious, words are mere metaphors for things. This is shown by the biting episode in Part III of *Gulliver's Travels* where the traveler reaches the city of Lagado and visits the Grand Academy. Here Dean Swift has the Projectors explain a plan to save our lungs by doing away with words in oral communication, "since words are only names for *things*, it would be convenient for all men to carry about them such things as were necessary to express the particular business they are to discourse on." This solution, along with prolonging our lives, would also eliminate the need for all the many languages that are spoken in the world. We could even get about rebuilding Babel. More than likely Swift was also hinting at class distinctions here, as a wealthy man with a retinue of servants carrying his "things" would be much more eloquent and expressive than a poor man who would have to do with one simple rucksack. In the real world the rich man with his college education can express himself so much better and more clearly than the poor illiterate.

There is more to it than this. If a word is a metaphor for a thing, why does a single thing have so many metaphors in orbit about it? Here we have the dire consequences of Babel. If Mama Lucy had speech, her *Ursprache* must have spread out and scattered into more variants than the birdsongs of a single species. This has left us with a welter of words to designate one simple *thing*. *Stone* can never sound like *pierre*, so are the two words interchangeable simply because they represent the same object? Since Flaubert would either say or think *pierre* when he picked one up does *stone* cover his thought when we translate him? We can only say that here translation has betrayed a complete and clear sense of the stone's thingness for the author, with no attempt in this lithic example to bring in the attendant nuances of Peter and the Papacy. That Lagadian discussion would best be left to the likes of Bouvard and Pécuchet, along with the analysis of why a diamond is a stone to the jeweler but a rock to the jewel thief.

Not only has the object been betrayed here but the word itself has also been. As it moves ahead (progresses?), a language will load a word down with all manner of cultural barnacles along the way, bearing it off on a different tangent from a word in another tongue meant to describe the same thing. Among languages there are ever so many terms used to denote the same object and by their very variety they beggar any possibility of ascertaining the unique reality of said object. The now regnant cult of indeterminacy might be happy with this, but *homo sapiens* likes to know as his name implies and which is what makes us what we are today and what we shall be tomorrow if we ever get that far. It may be that there is something like Heisenberg's principle of uncertainty at work in lexicology so that every time we call a stone a *pierre* we have somehow made it something different from a *stone* or a *Stein*. This leaves us with the question of whether a stone can ever be a *pierre* or a *pierre* a stone and whether either of them can be that hard object we are looking at on the ground, teaching us that even if a thing can be cloned the word that designates it cannot and any attempt to reproduce it in another tongue is betrayal.

Some concepts seem to be the exclusive property of one language and cannot be rightly conceived in another. When we have trouble coming up with just the right word in English we turn to the French and say "a certain *je ne sais quoi.*" If we say "a certain I don't know what" the effect is ragged and even unnatural. As we borrow from another language to enrich our own, more often than not there is treason afoot, if not in the meaning certainly in the sound. Although the French sound of *lingerie* is not too difficult to reproduce fairly closely in English, most people will *plusquam* it into a hyper-Gallic *lahnjeray*, a sound worthy of W. C. Fields and his *say finay*. A betrayal of language is many times the betrayal of words and at the same time it is a reflection of the hurdles present in communicating between cultures. We tend to acculturate foreign sensitivities, sensibilities, and reflexes into our own milieu with the requisite changes. Ask a New Yorker what Kafka's Gregor Samsa awoke as and the inevitable answer will be a giant cockroach, the insect of record in his city. What Kafka called it was simply an *ungeheuern Ungeziefer*, a monstrous vermin. He then goes on to describe what is obviously a hard-carapaced beetle. The pull of local reality is too strong for a New Yorker to make a closer concept or translation. This then can be seen as a betrayal by the imposition of another culture.

Most of these matters merge to form an indirect betrayal of the author. He is a compendium of all these factors. language, culture, and individual words. These are, in fact, inseparable, and the author is their product, the same as what he writes. His free will and originality only exist within the bounds of his culture. If he is to betray it, he betrays it from within, which connotes intimate knowledge, while the translator betrays it from without, from an acquired reflective, not reflexive, awareness.

Within his cultural limits the author, as an individual, can and, indeed, must extend himself as far as he can to set himself and his art apart from the commonplace, showing all the while whence he comes, doing this through language most of all. With the translator we have quite the opposite situation. He cannot and must not set himself apart from the culture laid out before him. To do so would indeed be treasonous. He must marshal his words in such a way that he does not go counter to the author's intent. Nowhere is translation more dubious than here as we try to translate into our own language and culture something that the author is translating into words within his culture and still make it our own. Treasonous it is. The important thing is to consider whether the treason is high or low, the sin mortal or venial. There are those who, like Nabokov, view translation as a criminal act that can only be judged as to whether it is a felony or just a misdemeanor and there are so many critics who do enjoy walking the perp.

While all this is going on, matters of which the translator must be quite aware, there is a danger of the translator's committing the saddest treason of all, betrayal of himself. The translator, we should know, is a writer too. As a matter of fact, he could be called the ideal writer because all he has to do is write; plot, theme, characters, and all the other essentials have already been provided, so he can just sit down and write his ass off. But he is also a reader. He has to read the text closely to know what it's all about. Here is where he receives less guidance or direction from the text. It is a common notion to say that if a work has 10,000 readers it becomes 10,000 different books. The translator is only one of these readers and yet he must read the book in such a way that he will be reading the Spanish into English as he goes along, with the result that his reading is also writing. His reading, then, becomes the one reading that is going to spawn 10,000 varieties of the book in the unlikely case that it will sell that many copies and will be read by that many people.

Our translator must know that this is the best he can do in this place and at this time and must still recognize that his work is, in a sense, unfinished. Although I have been satisfied with a translation when I finish it (as a translator ought to be), years later as I peruse the published text I find myself wishing I could make some changes for the better. When a translator starts an attempt at reasoning out a solution it is best to emulate Alexander before Phrygia as he sliced through the Gordian knot with his sword in a demonstration of what Ortega y Gasset called "vital reason." The translator must not betray his hunches. There will be carping from the critics, but he will be closer to being right that way and, in any case, he will not have betrayed himself. A careful confidence in himself is as necessary for a translator as it is for the point man in an infantry patrol. He must have a care, however, and remember that with the addition of a slightly aspirated letter *auteur* becomes *hauteur*.

The translator must put to good use that bugbear of timid technicians: the value judgment. In translation as in writing, which it is as we have said, the proper word is better than a less proper but standard one. Here again the translator must borrow Alexander's short sword. Translation is based on choice and a rather personal one at that. Long ago I discovered a funny thing: if you ponder a word, any word, long enough it will become something strange and meaningless and usually ludicrous. I suppose this is some kind of verbicide, bleeding the poor word of its very essences, its precious bodily fluids, and leaving a dry remnant that could pass for a five-letter group in a cryptographic message. When we snap out of it and retrieve the meaning of the word, we have, in a sense, deciphered it. This is as far as I would go in turning translation entirely over to reason since so much of it should be based on an acquired instinct, like the one we rely on to drive a car, Ortega's vital reason.

II

In Pursuit of Other Words

LET ME COMMIT AN ACT OF treason against myself now by confessing that translation was not a métier I had set out to follow, nor did I prepare myself for it with any conscious training or contemplation. The Spanish have a saying that goes "*El diablo sabe más por viejo que por diablo*" (The devil knows more from being old than from being the devil). I've come to realize lately that what I've been preening myself for as intelligence is simply the fact that I've been around too damned long as I restrain hubris and remember that Lear was old ere he was wise. I have always thought that I just stumbled into translation because it was there, serendipity, but with my wiser retrovision I can see that I harbored certain traits that fit nicely in with the needs of translation and which I have honed sharp through use.

I can trace my life back to a certain moment, an epiphany, if you will, when I came into complete self-awareness. From that moment on, existence has been a more or less continuous thread of memory, something that still makes me wonder as I contemplate it from this life of ours as schedule, with its hours, days, and years. I was about three years old and was walking back down Pinneo Hill road to the family house north of Hanover in New Hampshire. I don't know where I'd been

been or why, maybe to Damascus, but I was never as sure of myself as old Saul had been. Memory before that had been quite sporadic, as it has become once more over the years, bits and pieces recalled vaguely and episodically as from a dream. This was that odd period in existence when we are as strangers to our now selves. For most of any recall of what I had seen up to before that mystical revelation on Pinneo Hill I was beholden to my parents and others for any memory of what I had been doing. The gist of that period is nicely summed up by Chico Marx as Chicolini in *Duck Soup* when the prosecutor, played by Charles B. Middleton, asks him when he was born and Chico explains that he can't remember, he was just a little baby.

It is in this twilight consciousness that we first begin to listen and to speak. When I came into full self-awareness at three I was already endowed with speech and a fair vocabulary in English. Other tongues came later with conscious acquisition. At that existential awakening, however, as I returned home from I know not where up the hill, I seemed to have no conscious flow of memory of what I had been doing the day before and earlier. The mysterious part of that reverse Alzheimer's was the existence of certain words and names that I had coined during those previous days, the provenance of which was unknown to me and to everyone else. One of these has stayed with me as I have been reminded of it, and it continues to fascinate me. The word is *magotso*, or however it might be spelled, and it is evidently a word I would say when passing a cemetery. I am hard put to come up with a legitimate word for a graveyard that could have been mangled into this bizarre form by infantile efforts at speech. Could it have been some atavistic throwback to Adam who, according to Genesis, was given the marvelous creative privilege of naming things? Perhaps when the sad moment came to plant Abel. Or maybe it was something left over from what Lucy said. Yet again could there have been some early intimations of mortality brought on by my anticipation of getting to know Kierkegaard?

Then there was my first cat, a fine gray tabby queen whose descendants of all colors and types, depending on the wandering tom of the moment, came to inhabit the place for years to come. I must admit that at the time I thought the word "tabby" was, like "puss," a synonym for cat. We called that type a tiger cat. I had dubbed the animal Quidry, a nice Latinate name; where I'd got it from remains a mystery. It might have been some attempt to reproduce the cat's meow, which she also was. This seemingly unconscious christening was more fortunate than one that I undertook many, many years later during my conscious period. I'd come into possession of another fine tabby to share my cramped quarters on Sullivan Street in the Village. This one I named Catso, no doubt under the influence of the name Fatso. I should have known better, having served in Italy for two and a half years during the war. Most likely I simply wasn't aware of what I was doing, especially since there are differences in spelling, and southern Italians tend to voice the initial consonant.

These small personal anecdotes serve to show how words have any number of possible nuances for every individual as they rest in the subconscious and relate to some early experience. Mr. Chomsky might delve further into the possibility that we may be carrying some mysterious remote lexicon in our DNA. In the translation of words, then, the problem is compounded. We now have the personal word of the author's to be transformed into a personal word of the translator's. As always with translation, this calls for a choice among synonyms. Ideally the author's choice among the synonyms in his own language was made in a purposeful and conscious way. In most cases, however, and as it should be, it is made quite naturally and instinctively: "This is how I want to say it." The translator, too, should most usually work from this natural application of meaning: "This is how we say it in English." Nevertheless, the translator must be alert and aware of the fact that both he and the author have their "own" words. It seems easy to match like words (dog/*cão*) and proceed on. What *dog* connotes for me, however, is probably different from what *cão* suggests for António Lobo Antunes, although in common usage he must of course be satisfied with *cão* as I must be with *dog*.

This personal aspect of language can be extended to life itself. As far as the individual is concerned, life truly exists only as he feels it and thereby ponders it. It follows, therefore, that life is an idea, a word, in short, a metaphor for conscious existence and hence a translation. We are translating our existence and our circumstance as we go along living and before we are fatally assigned the translator's lot once the treason has been done: Segismundo's tower or tomb. We must also remember that "In the beginning was the Word, and the Word was with God, and the Word was God (John I:1). Even God as the Word has been put down and translated variously. The pensive Greeks call Him *logos* while the active Romans say *verbum*. So that even God, like existence, is an ambiguous translation, which could explain William James's varieties. When God's mystical name is finally articulated it, too, will have to be translated, unless we accept it as the acronym for Guaranteed Overnight Delivery which so blasphemously appears on certain trucks. Then there are those people hard of hearing who assert that God's name is, in fact, Howard, as in "Our Father which art in Heaven, Howard be thy name." I can't see how anyone could be an atheist with a God named Howard and it also might explain why the universe is such a mixed-up place.

Names are one of the bugbears of translation and usually illustrate its impossibility. Almost all Christian and Old Testament names have local versions wherever the Good Book is esteemed; Charles becomes Carlos; John, Juancito or Johnny, and so forth. These names are not only loaded down with ancient biblical or classical connotations but have acquired ever so many new ones along the way. Names, and especially nicknames, almost always carry some cultural nuance: a good-time Charley, a Johnny-come-lately, *Pedro por su casa*. For purposes of evacuation we go to the john; in Portugal one goes to have a talk with Miguel, or simply to the Miguel. This last name in familiar English is reduced to one syllable, Mike, while in Spanish it gains another, Miguelito. Can either one therefore ever be the equivalent of the other?

By not translating names we can at least maintain a certain aura of the original tongue and its culture. Spanish almost always translates royal names and sometimes those of famous commoners (Thomas More/Tomás Moro), while English is inconsistent. Shakespeare will be Guillermo in Spanish but Cervantes is always Miguel in English. English renders Carlos V and Felipe II as Charles V and Philip II although Alfonso XIII is never Alphonse. Having grown up hearing about Kaiser Wilhelm II in English I am still a bit befuddled when hearing Emperor William II from those farther removed in time from that worthy. Hitler to me was always Adolf but now I most often see Adolph and hear ay-dolf. In my own translations I prefer keeping names in the original while sometimes translating nicknames if they carry some descriptive value and can be translated without doing too much mischief to the tone of the story. Laurel and Hardy are better known in Spanish as El Gordo y el Flaco, corresponding to what children in my day used to call them: Fat and Skinny (I would be interested in knowing why it is in both languages that the epithets should reverse the order of the surnames). Roman names are largely maintained in English while the pronunciation is anglicized (i.e., If Julius Caesar sees her he will surely seize her), while in Spanish and French they are hispanized and gallicized (Julio César and Jules César). To my ear the English usage sounds properly alien and classical. Greek names often hold a Latinate form in English, cf. Herodotus.

I recently finished the translation of a novel by the Colombian Jorge Franco Ramos entitled *Rosario Tijeras*. Rosario, the main character, is nicknamed Tijeras (shears, scissors) because her earliest act of violence was to take her mother's sewing tool and geld the man who had raped her. Translating the epithet that had been hung on her would be awkward. Leaving it also followed in a certain way the old manner in which surnames were acquired. Her real name, like God's, is never revealed and everyone knew her as Rosario Tijeras. Nor does the nickname stand in need of translation as the episode wherein she acquires it is recounted early in the book.

Words, as well as certain idioms and grammatical usages, are in many ways the items most quickly subject to a kind of Darwinian evolutionary process, except that the natural selection here encountered appears to my mind to be less of a survival of the fittest than it is a kind of dumbing down to the lowest common denominator. This, of course, depends on what one considers the fittest to be. Populists would most likely disagree with me in this matter, but I have always maintained that *vox populi, vox Dei* is an open invitation to atheism. Beyond any qualitative considerations, there is the matter of

changing times, *autres temps, autres moeurs*. As one who has established a beachhead on the isle of Octogenaria (adjacent to
the island of Barataria), I have found that in many ways I am
what one might call "archaically active" or "actively archaic."
Certain words and usages have changed or appeared or died
out during my lifetime. I have noticed more and more that
gonna has become standard usage in presidential and high-level
parlance and I wonder how it would have sounded back in
1941 if FDR had said "We're gonna win the war." Also how is
it that *gonna* edges out *gwine* (too Uncle Remus?) and *gone*
(too Pogo?) or the British *geng*? There must be some answer
based on sound linguistic theory.

Translators, then, are placed in the difficult position of
having to be careful not to nail their translation onto the period in which they are living. If the work under way is something contemporary the effect won't be quite so bad since the
original text might well become archaic even sooner than
the translation. Like the leaves on trees, words age, yellow, and
drop off after a time, although languages, like trees, are divided
into different species and the words in one may hold their
meaning longer than those in the language into which they
are being translated. When I come to translate a "classic" I try
to find what we might call "evergreen" words. Translating
Machado de Assis, who wrote the most enduring Portuguese
since Camões (perhaps even more so, given the fact that he
was a novelist), I try hard to find words that are equally valid in
his time and in ours and which, we hope, will endure beyond
both ages. A good translation of Cervantes, and there are quite
a few, must not be so contemporary that it will eventually become archaic because Cervantes as read today in Spanish is
only mildly so. Motteux can sound archaic because he was a
contemporary of Cervantes, Putnam cannot. Where Motteux

messed up was in not finding as many evergreen words as Cervantes had used. Perhaps he didn't let Cervantes lead him linguistically. As I discovered translating Machado de Assis and García Márquez, the masters will enable you to render their prose into the best possible translation if you only let yourself be led by their expression, following the only possible way to go. If you ponder you will have lost the path.

III

STRINGING WORDS TOGETHER

BY CULTURE

WE HAVE SEEN THE WILD variety of meanings, subtle and direct, that cling to words. We have also considered the perils and impossibilities of metaphor as we go from one language to another. This morass of troubles is made all the more swampy as we come to the task of joining these translated words together to make sense in the new language. This process must take into account what is called syntax, grammar, and the like, as all the pitfalls we had to confront with individual words are not only encountered here but a good many new ones as well. Cultures are at work again. Word order that seems quite logical to one people will look absurd to another. So-called dialect comedians have used this phenomenon to great advantage in their skits since so much of comedy and humor is based on absurdities. Our own language itself can seem absurd when placed under a neutral light. If we stare at a word long enough it will become strange and even foolish, to the ruination of any sense it might have had before. Absurdities exist within our own language when we become hyper-correct, as shown by Winston Churchill's mocking of a copyeditor's correction, commenting that "This is something up with which I will not put."

For older evidence of what annoyed Churchill we have the development of the Romance languages from Latin. As schoolboys and girls we had to struggle with the makeup of Greek and Latin. I think that Latin was harder, even if Greek did have its strange first and second aorists (only matched later on by Russian and its aspects). But we were studying that noble and complex tongue of Cicero and Virgil, not the language of the marketplace. The assorted Celtic, Iberian, Italic, and other hewers of wood and drawers of water had already made the Latin language more pliable to their simple needs as evinced by the language of their church in the Vulgate. The people were well on their way to getting rid of case endings and simplifying the system of tenses as what were to be new languages evolved. It really must pain the French in their linguistic hubris to realize that they are really speaking bad Latin. And, yet, these various supposedly inept versions of the Latin language have produced beautiful bits of expression that can belong only to them. For all of his wonderful lines it is impossible to imagine Ovid's coming out with something like Verlaine's "*Les sanglots longs des violons de l'automne.*" I contend that the sound of a language must come from the cultural expression and evolution of a people. Only a Frenchman can properly mouth the poetry of Verlaine in a way that is completely natural and even instinctive because the rendition comes from that part of his brain wherein his native language is housed. It has been claimed that a person who has lost his speech because of a stroke can still communicate in a foreign language he may have learned because it is lodged in a different portion of his brain (a very telling argument for learning another language). If this be so, then we are faced with the possibility that when we shift into another language we become a different person by running on a different part of our brain. So the poor translator must not just go back and forth between two languages, but if he is worthy of his calling must shift between two selves, with all the perils of this induced schizophrenia.

The matter of subject, verb, and object, therefore, and their placement in a sentence will depend on the cultural instincts of the language spoken. Heavy-handed humorists often avail themselves of syntactical differences between languages in order to make fun of them. This is usually accompanied by a burst of macaronic pronunciation. But Romance languages have, in certain ways, been an improvement over classical Latin as vehicles for easier communication with their elimination of case endings and a resort to prepositions in order to denote re-lationships. At the same time they did away with Latin's ability to make words fit certain poetical meters in a way that be-comes a quite natural rhythmical performance. Modern at-tempts to follow this too closely in translation are usually clumsy and Procrustean. It all adds up to Robert Frost's com-monplace regarding the relationship between poetry and its translations, but that comment of his could well apply to prose as well. In even the best of examples a translation cannot get to the marrow of what has been said in the original. A piece of writing cannot be cloned in another language, only imitated. Like the colors of the spectrum, languages are unique and dis-tinctive; they can approach each other but never reproduce one another. Columbia's blue can never reproduce Yale's, yet both are blue and have a great many cultural concomitants in common. What makes translation seem so possible is that we live in a world of similarities and it is too much with us. Lan-guages, like the colors mentioned above, are similar and we can at least imagine how they would look in another hue. But what about those invisible colors that lurk at the ends of the spectrum? The limits of our ability to perceive show up in the fact that we are unable even to imagine what these colors might be like. We would have to be certain birds. Translation may be impossible, but it can at least be essayed.

IV

IN THE BEGINNING

SERENDIPITY HAS BEEN THE mainstay of my life as it has no doubt been that of countless other existences. Things just seem to fall together. My full-fledged entry into translation came about in such a way. After the war and the army in 1945 I felt that I ought to recoup some of the relaxing academic time lost to military service. I was meant to be graduated in the class of 1944, but in 1942 I enlisted in the Army Reserves. When I was called up I lacked but six points toward a diploma, having taken my comprehensive exams after some extra courses and a couple of summer sessions. With this behind me, Dartmouth was good enough to award me my degree while I was still overseas. I gathered that I had been given three points of physical education for infantry training and three points of modern European history for OSS, as we were making quite a bit of it at the time. So it was that I wandered up to Morningside Heights to see what Columbia had to offer. I'd thought of the School of Journalism, but there was too much legwork and interviewing involved. I also turned down the Law School; too much of a grinding existence and I wanted some R and R. So I ended up in the Graduate Faculties in the Department of Spanish and Portuguese, having been a Romance Languages major in college with more Spanish than French on my transcript.

I wasn't sure what I was going to do with my Master's degree, which I got in 1947. I wrote on the poetry of Miguel de Unamuno. I had wanted to write on Antonio Machado, but my mentor, Don Angel del Río, told me that much had been written on Machado and that a study of Unamuno would be a real contribution. What I discovered from it all was that Unamuno was a fascinating and strange figure of a man but that Machado's poetry was ever so much better. I had no real notion of going into teaching, wondering what to do next, when Don Federico de Onís, our chairman, offered me a part-time position, which I accepted. I had just taken an apartment on Morton Street in the Village (on that short, grubby part of otherwise tony Morton Street between Seventh Avenue and Bleecker) and the job would go farther toward paying the rent, a princely $27.50 per month, than my maintenance under the G.I. Bill. I'd had no thoughts about going on for what seemed to me to be that out-of-reach doctorate, but by then I gathered that it was the thing to do. The result was a dissertation on black characters in Brazilian fiction. I switched from Spanish to Portuguese because there was more room to roam there and I liked what I had studied of the language in college. Brazil also held a certain fascination for me, maybe because it was so different from the run-of-the-mill areas I could have studied. Thus, in 1948 I became a full-time instructor in Columbia College and was off and away on what looked like a career I'd never imagined a few years before and which was to lead me into other equally unimagined activities.

By that time I had quite a few good friends at Columbia. One of these was Alan Purves, an English instructor whom I got to know as a colleague in the Humanities A (Great Books) course that we taught and also as a fellow proctor during Law School exams, where impecunious instructors could pick up some needed change along with a bit of impressive legal lingo as we read the exam questions. It seemed that Alan, in collaboration with Ursula Eder and Saul Galin of Brooklyn College, was putting together a literary review that was to be called *Odyssey*. A quarterly, it would cover contemporary writing from two European and two Latin American countries in each issue. I was asked to sign on as the editor in search of new writing in Spanish and Portuguese. The work was rather pleasant and none too onerous as I pored over recently arrived issues of literary journals at the 42nd Street library. I found a lot of things and, of course, they had to be translated. That was where it all started. I made quite a few translations under a series of fanciful pseudonyms in order to give an impression of variety. (I had to withhold the temptation to use Mahatma Kane Jeeves.) What amazed me later on was the number of authors I translated whose work would come before me afterward for translation for established publishers. *Odyssey* was the true forerunner of what in the United States would subsequently be called the Latin American "Boom." As has been the case with so many worthy pioneering efforts, we were ahead of our time. That other boom, the foundation explosion, hadn't occurred yet. The magazine, handsome as it was, had been started on the proverbial shoestring, with no salaries and with a wink at royalty payments in some cases. In spite of enthusiastic comments received, we folded after six issues. But we were left with a lasting feeling of satisfaction as we saw so many of our unknown authors go on to receive Nobels and worldwide acclamation.

It was during this time that I received a summer fellowship for travel to Brazil under the auspices of anthropologist Charles Wagley's Institute of Latin American Studies at Columbia. I was now teaching a course in Portuguese, and I was going to Brazil to hone my fluency, meet literary people, and buy books for the Columbia library. I landed in Brazil at Belém, by the mouth of the Amazon, and as I lounged in the lobby of the Grande Hotel watching questionable characters come and go, I was waiting for Walter Slezak to appear at any moment under the ceiling fans in his rumpled suit and a straw hat as he went about some sort of illicit business.

From there it was to Recife and its airport next to the village with the beautifully apt name of Boa Viagem. It was in Recife that my literary trip began. I sought out the American cultural attaché at the consulate to see about arranging a meeting with the sociologist Gilberto Freyre, author of *The Masters and the Slaves*, whom I'd met at Columbia in Frank Tannenbaum's seminar. The attaché asked me if I would like to meet a young writer from Rio who was in town mother-henning a touring university theatrical group. I was delighted, as she was when I invited her to come along with me to see Gilberto, whom she'd never met. This was Nélida Piñon, who has become one of Brazil's best novelists and the first woman president of the Brazilian Academy of Letters. She has been a close friend ever since.

From Recife I went to Bahia (Salvador to outsiders) and was disappointed to find Jorge Amado out of town. I did manage to visit his haunts, however, which could be useful in future translations, and I had lunch at his favorite restaurant, Maria de São Pedro's, over a barbershop through which you entered. It would burn down a few years later in the disastrous dockside fire. Bahia, the colonial capital of Brazil, is also the great center of Afro-Brazilian culture. I was able to take in a non-tourist *candomblé* and I also got to see some *capoeira* before both became Disneyfied.

Then it was on to Rio where I saw Nélida again. She took me to any number of *lançamentos*, as book parties are called. I became acquainted with a goodly number of writers and literary figures including Antônio Houaiss, who would translate Joyce's *Ulysses* for a handsome sum that was the equivalent of five hundred dollars. While American translators at the time were doing what amounted to charitable work, their Brazilian compeers were even worse off.

I'd been hauling a copy of my dissertation along with me and was referred to a young man who worked at the Institute for African Studies named Eduardo Portella. He was interested and I left him the thesis to read. Not long after my return home I had a letter from him telling me that he wanted to publish the book. It seems that he'd gone off on his own in the meantime and had started a journal called *Tempo Brasileiro* and a publishing house of the same name. As was the case with Nélida, Eduardo and I became good friends. The last time I saw him was when my wife Clem and I were delegates to the International PEN Congress in Rio, where he was receiving everyone as Minister of Education during the *glasnost* regime of General Figueiredo, the last of Brazil's military presidents.

Columbia got its books and I brought back a great number of my own. Among them was a collection of short, short stories by Dalton Trevisan, a writer from Curitiba. One story of his, "The Corpse in the Parlor," was so much to the *noir* taste shared by Saul Galin and me that we put it in *Odyssey*. It would reappear later in a collection of his stories which I translated for Knopf under the title *The Vampire of Curitiba and Other Stories*. Over the years I was in correspondence with Dalton and I would watch as his new items got shorter and shorter. He said it was his aim to keep on trying until he wrote the ultimate haiku. Most of his stories deal with a couple called João and Maria, who are engaged in what he calls "the conjugal war."

Back at Columbia patience and Portuguese brought me tenure, that *rara avis* in our department. It was then, as I savored memories of Brazil, that serendipity struck again. I got a phone call from Sara Blackburn at Pantheon Books asking if I might be interested in translating a novel by the Argentinean writer Julio Cortázar. It was *Rayuela*, which was to appear in English as *Hopscotch*. I had heard of Cortázar but hadn't read the book. This didn't prevent me from accepting the offer. Still without having read the entire book, I submitted the two sample chapters requested. Both Sara and Julio liked my version so I signed a contract to do my first translation of a long work for a commercial publisher. It was the start of a career I hadn't sought after and the beginning of a beautiful friendship with the incomparable Julio. True to my original instincts (or perhaps my inherent laziness and impatience) and to the subsequent amazement of those to whom I confessed my hubristic ploy, I translated the book as I read it for the first time. Even though it might have been a matter of that casual laziness, with time I have managed to convince my own Pyrrhonian self that it was precisely the way Julio meant it to be done. When I finished the novel it seemed very much like that.

This would become my usual technique with subsequent books. I used the excuse that it gave the translation the freshness that a first reading would have and which ought to make others' reading of the translation be endowed with that same feeling. I have put forth this explanation so many times that I have come to believe it, loath as I am to confess that I was just too lazy to read the book twice. I do think, really, that by doing things this way I was birthing something new and natural and wouldn't have to shout with Colin Clive, "It's alive! It's alive!" Of course it was, from the very beginning. It was gestated, not assembled out of dead parts, or something reconstructed after being deconstructed by analysis.

When the translation came out it got a positive review on the front page of *The New York Times Book Review* by Donald Keene. I was naturally pleased by an approving comment on the translation, so often missing in reviews. I had gone back to Brazil by then to do research under a Fulbright grant on that wild Luso-Brazilian missionary and visionary Padre Antônio Vieira. Soon after my return home I had the good news that my translation had won the first National Book Award for Translation, which was later dropped, sad to say. I was off and away. If I had turned right instead of left at any number of junctures in my life none of this would have happened and I would have been doing something else. Serendipity.

V

ME AND MY CIRCUMSTANCE

ORTEGA Y GASSET FAMOUSLY DEFINED the individual by saying *"Yo soy yo y mi circunstancia"* (I am I and what's around me). Although I may have said that I sort of backed into translation without having thought about it or having set my sights on it, I do have within me certain ingredients, innate or circumstantial, that could be said to have tilted me in that direction. Many far-flung genes have come to rest in my being, given the fact that my grandparents were born in four different countries: Spain, Cuba, England, and the United States. My Catalan grandfather married his Cuban-born niece and Andrew Maverick Macfarland of New York married Kate Mosley of the Manchester clan, although she must also be claimed as a New Yorker, having arrived here at the age of six or such. I'm never sure whether the pithy remarks she has handed down come from Lancaster or the streets of her adopted city. The Macfarlands go back a few generations; their arrival from Scotland is vague. Great-grandfather Thomas Mott Macfarland married Ann Maverick and although she was not of the cattle-breeding branch, many of her descendants have shown tendencies of an unbranded existence. These, then, are my genetic circumstances, which are coupled to a set of geographical ones that are equally piebald.

I was born in Yonkers, but they didn't fit so I moved away. What had happened was that my father, the Cuban sugar broker Miguel Rabassa, had married Clara Macfarland, the lass out of Hell's Kitchen, begotten three sons, and then lost his wad; almost all of it, that is. The big house on Park Hill in Yonkers, where true love had really conquered, was gone, along with one of his two Cadillacs and Charlie the chauffeur and his brother Rudy the footman. Fortunate for all, especially for me, was the fact that, land-poor now, my father had been able to hang on to his thousand-acre farm in Hanover, New Hampshire, four miles north of Dartmouth College. That is where I grew up.

The farm had a herd of prize Ayrshire cattle, a breed unusual in those parts, as well as the usual chickens, pigs, and assorted dogs and cats. The farm wasn't to last long, however, as it had been more of a show place than a commercial enterprise. The cows, horses, and equipment were all sold off, and with the addition of a large dining room the big house became the Villaclara Inn, a slight change in the name of Villa Clara Farm. At that point my existence settled down, just as I was turning six and starting school. The year was 1928 and we were soon to have many fellow-sufferers in relative penury. Some of the first bits of political terminology I learned were things like Prohibition (pronounced pro'bition), Depression, Hoovervilles, and Hoover tourists (hoboes). My father was of an adventurous nature and he dabbled in sheep, chickens, and even fried plantain chips, none of which took off commercially. He would follow the Market, as it was singly and simply called then to the exclusion of any other exchange, and mutter about what he could do if he only had a thousand dollars.

Both my parents were good word people. As a foreigner and especially as a Cuban one, my father not only had become fluent in English but would fool around with it as only someone with an outside vantage point could. My mother had brought with her the lingo of Hell's Kitchen New York and also her mother's colorful parlance, partly from Manchester but mainly from an older New York. As the youngest child of many, my mother had also learned a lot of terms and talk from her older siblings. Our childhood nicknames evolved into strange forms as the years went by. Miss Emma Macfarland, a maiden aunt and former schoolteacher who had become somewhat disarranged upstairs, had come to live with us and help out as best she could. She had her own terms of endearment for my brothers and me: Dootsus-Wootus was my brother Jerome (also known as Dito or Deet, wherein lies another tale of nomenclature), Obsty-Bobsty was brother Bob, and I was Gozy-Wozy. These became shortened to the first part and were taken up by other family members. As a baby my brother Jerome had evidently resembled someone on the Cuban side and had elicited the comment *"dito cagadito"* (roughly "the shit and image"). On leaving home he became Jerry to his friends but was still Deet to the family.

In a similar way I began as Geg or Gegs at home to become Greg on the outside. My mother always called me Gegs and my brother Bob knew me as Geg. Jerome later on called me Greg but he was always Deet to me. My best nickname evolved out of a radio show I would listen to. I was a great admirer of Indians and always their defender, most likely from my love of nature but also from a fascination with things exotic. It was Chief Wolfpaw's program and there was a club which I joined for a certain number of cereal boxtops, no doubt. I received a pin in the shape of an arrowhead with the spoor of a wolf's paw embedded on it. The club's password was Ho-wa-ho-so-wa-ka, which I would go about mouthing, to the amusement of my father, whose version mutated into Mahokey-mazokey. Uncle George Macfarland picked up on this and reduced it to Mazoke, a nickname he used for me to the end of his days.

Another Macfarland who lived with us after quitting his job as a letter carrier in New York because of a heart condition was Uncle Andrew (he never used Junior). In addition to the inn, we had a filling station and sometime lunchroom a quarter of a mile up the road on the bank of the Connecticut River. This was his realm. His nickname was Ayza, which for a long time I thought was just a voiced version of Asa. Much later I learned that it was a childhood epithet hung on him because he was given to telling people to "kiss me ayza." Here was another one who liked to play with words and had maintained his Hell's Kitchen accent all through his years of exile in New Hampshire's frigid Cocytus. It has been my observation that this so-often mocked and maligned manner of speech which, alas, can be heard today only in old movies is never the "foist" that bumpkins think they've heard, but a softer sound, more like the German *eu* with just a hint of the missing *r*. In this it is rather close to Oxbridge, except that it's much too bumptious to be mumbled as an indistinct "waffle-waffle" as Herbert Marshall might.

With all the diverse mannerisms of speech I heard around me, including the various differing New England ones, I developed what might be called an ear for sounds. I had fun imitating and perfecting these different accents, using them in high-school plays and just fooling around. Once I even passed myself off as an Englishman to a poor student teacher in one of our classes. All along I'd been curious about languages. My father had an *Encyclopedia Britannica* in one of those famous early editions. The articles on countries would include a section on language. I remember going through it trying to pick up a phrase here and there. Later on I was pleased to find that some of them were authentic, although others verged on the pidgin. Strangely, I didn't pick up much Spanish at home, most likely because my father spoke English most of the time, except when there might be a Cuban friend or a Spanish-speaking Dartmouth student about. José Clemente Orozco came by for some *arroz con pollo* when he was painting his famous murals in the reserve reading room of Baker Library (I remember hearing a tourist some years later inquiring as to where she might find the Orezco frescoes). My active ear was pleased no end with that malapropism. My father did use his Spanish when he was in need of an immediate expletive, however, and if he came to cut himself while working in the kitchen he would deliver himself of what José Rubén Romero's Pito Pérez called *un carajo rotundo y retumbante.* He would also curse in English, less instinctively reactive, however, and usually adjectival, like his favorite "God-dem."

Formal language training began for me in high school with Latin and French, the only ones offered. In college I made an early switch in majors from chemistry/physics to Romance languages, starting Spanish and continuing French. I soon developed into a language collector with my first course in Portuguese with good Joe Folger, who had picked it up early from fishermen on his native Nantucket. As I was about to start German the Soviet Union was invaded and Russian was offered as a wartime option. I put off German until after the war at graduate school. I guess I hadn't spent all my class time gazing at lovely Miss Alma Whitford, fresh out of Mount Holyoke, as she taught us to construe Caesar, because later on when I did more Latin in graduate school, what I had thought had disappeared was still there and in pretty good shape. I sat in on George Woods's Italian class and his Dante course, which would later serve me when I got to Italy. In Naples I found a splendid edition of the *Commedia* which would follow me up the peninsula and help me build up my Italian and get rid of Spanish and Portuguese intruders.

All through school and college I was doing translation as it was an important ingredient in language study in those days. It was a valuable exercise in building up vocabulary, especially at that early age when the brain's powers of retention were still strong. Old traditions still held because when I brought home my first French textbook, *Le Nouveau Chardenal*, my mother remarked that she had used that same book in high school. I wonder where they got off calling it *nouveau*. In those early days I was also well served by my ear for sounds. I had started piano lessons but never got beyond Diller/Quail, to my father's probable disappointment, although he never expressed any. On a Boy Scout camporee I'd tripped and broken a wrist and when the cast came off I never went back to the piano. Ever since, I've been limited to the role of listener, even though a rather avid and earnest one. Many years later, however, as a kind of recompense, I couldn't resist a bugle sitting in the window of an army-navy store in Saratoga Springs. I can now blow a semblance of the cavalry charge as well as Gunga Din's warning call, complete with the descending fadeout. I have since toyed with the idea of composing a Call for Papers to go with all those notices one gets for impending academic conferences. In the woods, where I spent some of my happiest times with my dogs, I got to recognize bird calls and could even imitate some. I was also pretty good at reproducing barnyard sounds. My cock's crow was much more authentic than either the English cock-a-doodle-doo or the Spanish qui-qui-ri-qui, both of which show the essential impossibility of translation.

Words and names were all around me. I had private nicknames for people which I never expressed or revealed because
their accuracy might be taken for cruelty or disdain, which
it was not. I would also look at the structure and window
arrangement of houses, giving them faces and making them, to
my mind's eye and ear, speak the names of their owners. This
seemed so foolish that I never mentioned it to anyone. The
private sphere we inhabit is largely secret, else we would reveal
it more often. My feeling is that this may hold the deepest instincts we put to use when we translate, before we lard it over
with reason and its concomitant rational attributes. These
latter, of course, are absolutely essential to our craft, yet, as in
life itself, a balance must be maintained. I might be the last one
ever to sense or seek out any mystical urges this side of the
Singularity, but the foolish and yet positive inclinations of our
mysterious mental ways must be followed. I think that these
seemingly somnambulistic musings of my early years have
been good for my application of thought to language and
from there, in reverse, to the language and thought of someone I have been translating.

My dabbling in languages in college came to a halt when
the reserves were called up and I went into the army. Before
that I had been interviewed by Bob Lang, an alumnus and former factotum at Dartmouth, for an organization called the
Office of Strategic Services, of which I had never heard, as be-
fitted its secret nature. I was told, along with several others,
that we should let him know when we were activated and he
would have us transferred to Washington. The next stop after
call-up was the reception center at Fort Devens, Massachu-
setts, where we would await assignment to other duties and
training. Bob Lang was notified, but nothing happened. As
time went on, people from our group were being shipped out

until by some queer quirk or reason my college roommate Al Hormel and I were the only ones left. Duty at Devens was not particularly strenuous as we went about various chores at the base, and I picked up army expressions and ways, most of which were not particularly noble or ennobling. It did much for my contemporary vocabulary, however, and it was also a badge of tribal separation from the alien civilian world on the outside, whose inhabitants would come to be known as "God-damned civilians." I could never enter the lodge-brother spirit of this as I still felt myself a member of that outside world, one who'd been hijacked out of it. Only after basic training (we didn't call it boot camp, it was "basic") did I feel myself a natural-born soldier.

There were two types of parlance that I encountered in the army. The first was official military-speak, which to my still-civilian ear seemed backwards and silly, as in "gloves wool olive drab." The second was soldier-speak, much more colorful and inventive, such as the embellishment "buck-ass private," and all the many FU's, some of which like SNAFU have passed into general speech, although there are those today like many of my young students who haven't the foggiest idea of what it stands for. I remember the posted outcome of some court-martial proceedings that combined the two aspects into a delightful linguistic merger. It seems that a soldier had been brought up on charges of insubordination and the specific charge said in part: ". . . and upon being reprimanded by Sgt. [So-and-So] did call Sgt. [So-and-So] a mother-fucking son-of-a-bitch or words to that effect." The intriguing problem is trying to ascertain what other words might have had that same effect.

Al and I were finally sent off to Camp Fannin, Texas, where we underwent infantry basic three successive times. The rigors of this were such that Bob Lang in Washington was in receipt of fervent pleas. He had commented that we had been chosen because of our cryptic minds. We wired him that those cryptic minds were going fast and to get us out of there. At long last orders were cut for our transfer to OSS Washington. Al Hormel was in charge of our two-man delegation because his name preceded mine in the alphabet. Among his instructions were thoroughgoing ones that detailed how to dispose of the remains of any member who might have succumbed en route.

In Washington we were assigned to the message center to learn cryptography in all its various phases. Here was another experience in language, albeit an artificial one. This brought to mind the figure of Pete Weston, a classmate and another language collector. Not satisfied with all the foreign tongues he had gathered in and learned well, Pete invented one of his own. As I think about it now I feel that it could be the basis for a test in translation. Why not make up your own language and then translate something from it into your native tongue, faithfully and making note of all difficulties you might come across? Then you could reverse the process and see if your new language is adequate for the translation of your native tongue. This reminds us of the fun you can have trying to translate mysterious languages: pre-Rosetta hieroglyphics or those strange runes inscribed on New York streets by Con Edison to pass on some arcane instructions telling wire crews where dig they must.

Our cryptographic work was rather elementary, consisting essentially in the decoding of incoming traffic and the encoding of the outgoing. We even had machines to do our work for us, as Billie Holiday used to sing, but it was a bit more than pushing the button on the wall. A typewriter was connected to a machine with rotors and this Big Bertha, as we called it, would decode five-letter groups which would then be typed out in clear text on the automatic typewriter. The process could be reversed as the rotors were changed and adjusted for security.

Not too long afterward I was posted to Algiers, still in the company of Al Hormel. The transfer gave me a chance to practice my French, but I never had a chance to learn any Arabic or Berber because the French maintained a fairly thorough though unofficial form of apartheid. I did get to speak some Spanish, however, with veterans of the Spanish Civil War who were living as refugees in the Bab-el-Oued district, some of whom worked in our mess tent. It was in Algiers that I began translating in a different sort of way. At that time our agents in the field were using a primitive double transposition cipher for their message. We called it DT. This system was simply a rearrangement of the letters in a message according to a set of indicators that could be carried in the head, usually a literary quotation. If the clear text of this system were to get out, the whole arrangement would be in danger. Before leaving the message center, therefore, the clear text of the message had to be rewritten, paraphrased, as we called it. This meant, in other words, translating from English into English.

So there I was, doing what I would be doing years later, not aware that I was already doing translation. As they would say today, the parameters were narrow. You didn't have the option of simply reworking the word order; the same letters would still be there. Sometimes it was hard to find good synonyms. There are words that have none and can't be resaid in some roundabout way. This was especially true if the message concerned order of battle, as so many did. A regiment had to be a regiment, a division a division, and their identifying numbers had to remain the same. Paraphrasing has something quite devious and even dishonest about it, like anything that has to do with intelligence and counter-intelligence. Might not this be the way with translation as well?

As Fifth Army advanced so did the 2677th Regiment OSS (Prov), from Algiers to Caserta, Italy, and thence to Rome near war's end. After the German surrender in Italy, which was largely an OSS matter (Operation Sunrise, why I don't know), people were being shipped home on their way to the Far East, my old comrade Al Hormel among them. As I had become message-center chief by then I stayed on, with no more war and all of Italy and a fair-sized motor pool at my disposal. It was then that I became a tourist, revisiting with more leisure places I had visited under less inviting circumstances. I also read my Dante and other items picked up along the way, honing my self-taught Italian to a passable fluency.

All this could have been called preparation for what I would be doing later, translating. Had I begun with such a far-sighted aim in mind I would have done ever so many things differently and might have ended up a knee-jerk, pedantic, post-modern craftsman. It was my good fortune, therefore, to have been left adrift in my circumstances, picking things up in an offhand way, a fun-loving Rover Boy (Tom, if memory serves) in the natural scene, what some might call the modernist incarnation of reality. There, then, is the explication of my translating.

VI

ADVANCE TO BE RECOGNIZED

MOST TRANSLATORS, MYSELF INCLUDED, have fallen victim at one time or another to a kind of paranoia, the feeling that there exists a hostile host of critics out there lying in wait for the proper moment to pounce upon us and savage what we have done. In recent times, however, translators have come to band together in various ways to counter the different ills and injustices that have befallen them. They have gathered in organized groups for both protection and mutual comfort as well as looking after the profession itself. For many years PEN American Center has maintained a Translation Committee whose business it is to shield translators from the depredations of unscrupulous publishers by proffering a model contract, which has begun to be followed more and more over the years. The committee also sponsors any number of literary events dealing with translation as well as awards prizes in different categories of translated works. It is unsparing of publishers and critics who neglect to mention the translator's name in a review or in advertising copy.

Many times the publisher's defense is part of his huckstering as he puts forth the argument that people won't buy a book if they know it's a translation. This argument, the sad result of the bottom line's having become the bottom line, is patently untrue, "the thing that is not," as Swift's Houyhnhnms would have put it. There are a fair number of foreign books that have sold well even with the translator's name boldly in view. The American reading public isn't completely made up of those whom Mencken skewered so mercilessly and in most cases quite accurately. In keeping with his position I would say that you'll never go broke underestimating the intelligence or overestimating the greed of a large portion of the publishing "community." Translators have most often been better served by the smaller houses, which are a reflection of that earlier age when the name Knopf on the spine of a book meant that the grand old Alfred himself also had his name on the door of his office and kept close watch on what was being published in other countries.

Along with the PEN committee we now have other groups in which translators have banded together and gained greater recognition. Two of these are the ATA (American Translators Association) and ALTA (American Literary Translators Association). The first is made up largely of commercial and technical translators but it also has an active literary section. ALTA has been quite successful in furthering the cause. Its gatherings have of necessity taken place most often in academic surroundings, a fact that has concerned the founders, who have feared the taint of professorial pedantry. I do think, however, that there have been some positive consequences of this with the rather widespread growth of writing courses dealing with translation. I've done some of this work myself as I've tried to teach what is unteachable. As I have said before, you can explain how translation is done, but how can you tell a student what to say without saying it yourself? You can tell him what book to read but you can't read it for him. It's my notion, loose as it might be, that when I'm translating a book

I'm simply reading it in English. The further technicalities, many of which I have obviously missed, are taken care of by the copyeditor. These are the writers who will perfect the work. There are translators who curse and demean the copyeditor, but I myself have great respect for her (I use the feminine because in my early days the copyeditor was most often a bright, young, hard-working, underpaid Smithie or Cliffie with the fresh glow of a major in English).

ALTA was probably right in its wish to avoid academia. In order to bring in their babies' bread most translators must have an academic connection and must toil in those insidious groves where translation, along with the rest of literature, has fallen into the hands of the big kids, who like to take things apart to see how they work. I remember the big kids as the spoilers, always ruining what the more imaginative little kids were up to. This activity is called deconstruction, unbuilding, and I refer those in the business to the episode in *One Hundred Years of Solitude* where old José Arcadio Buendía dismantles and then reassembles the pianola according to his own lights and the resultant weird cacophony. Pathologists call it dissection, but in either case there seems little hope for a proper reconstruction. Victor Frankenstein tried it and look what it got him. A work of art is a unit, it is the result of a vision, an insight, something we might call unutterable even when the creation is made up of words. In cryptography we speak of garbles when a message has gone awry. No amount of reconstruction will avail, only a construction, which has its seat in the imagination.

Too often the review of a translated book is assigned to a person whose field is the literature of the language involved. This character is the one Sara Blackburn so neatly dubbed Professor Horrendo. After he has dealt with the work in question, he will then roll up his sleeves and proceed to slice into the translation. His glee is almost visible. When alternatives are suggested they are inevitably of the tin-ear variety. These are people who would improve things by whitewashing Vermeer's yellow wall. Other reviewers will simply judge the flow of the English prose (poetry is too fugitive to go into here and I've written more of it than I've translated). Positive terms like "smooth," "flowing," and such are used along with negative ones like "awkward," "clumsy," and others. I have even seen "efficient," whatever that might mean, but that was delivered by the same pedantic twerp who had gone tooth and nail after a translation of mine without realizing that he was reading un-corrected proofs. This varied cohort makes up what Alastair Reid calls the translation police. In doing so I think he must have police brutality in mind rather than law and order.

The recognition I treasure most is the one coming from the authors themselves. García Márquez is said to have remarked that he liked my English version of *One Hundred Years of Solitude* better than his own original Spanish one. I can only humbly as-sume that the credit lies with the English language, that the book should have been written in English and I was only trying to correct that mistake. My mystical feeling, however, is that Gabo already had the English words hiding behind the Spanish and all I had to do was tease them out. Against this, however, is the fact that when I reluctantly reread my translation I keep see-ing things that I should have done better by.

Julio Cortázar, my first author and oldest friend among them all, liked the way I handled his stuff and anointed me with the title and status of Cronopio. Of all "my" authors he was the one who came closest to what might be called collab-oration. His marginal notes were well-taken and sometimes he would even alter his text to better fit the English. In one case the change was due to my typewriter's intransigence (unless Archie the cockroach had snuck in during the night and done his bit). The sentence was describing a fried egg that had been left in a pan on the stove for a week or two. For its sins my machine had typed "fired egg" instead of "fried egg." Julio said, "I like it. Let's keep it." He'd spotted the ceramic state of an egg left to idle that long. I was disappointed in a way that no Professor Horrendo or translation policeman was forthcoming to rant about that inaccuracy which Julio had thought was a creative improvement so I could have had the opportunity of straightening out his crooked way.

Translation has been fortunate these days to be surrounded by what is called multiculturalism, faddish though it may be. This effort at inclusiveness has let some questionable partners into the tent, but it has increased an awareness of other places and other ways. Strangely, I have not seen any great increase in the study of foreign languages (other tongues, they would like me to say, *nihil mihi alienum* and all that) in the schools or elsewhere. The great paradox is that this interest in the multiplicity of customs had moved along side by side with an increase in the hegemony of the English language and reversed baseball caps. For the moment translation is being aided by the attraction of other cultures, but if the dominance of English persists it will become the lingua franca and translation will become unnecessary as other languages become the province of scholars of an antique past.

This has already come to pass in many ways over recent years as generations succeed each other and new norms are established. Right now the number of translations brought out by the major (now commercialized) houses has dwindled down to scarcity, all in full view of the great cult of multiculturalism. Another strange phenomenon is the fact that as translations diminish on the popular market the number of translators busy with their most often worthwhile projects has increased. This certainly cannot be because a lucrative calling has attracted more people to its ranks. Since translations, unlike textiles, can't be farmed out for profit to needy people in poor countries, the money-publishers must pay at least what passes for adequate wages. It's a buyer's market, however, and given the needs of the ego to see one's work in print, the translator usually caves in. ATA did attempt to recommend a scale of pay and was immediately threatened with a monstrous and ruinous lawsuit for restraint of trade by a government that listens to the call of greed and screed. Rates have kept pace with inflation but they haven't moved much ahead of it. I can remember that when I first began, contracts would speak in terms of payment for a thousand words, which made the pay sound ever so lordly although the actual rate per lowly word would be in pennies. I had thought of installing some sort of device like a pedometer on my typewriter which would record every hit on the space bar so I could tell how much I'd made so far, but that attitude was better suited to the other camp.

Things are not so bad, however, and as I have said, workshops in translation have sprung up all over the academic world. It has become a favorite subject of studies purporting to seek a theory of the craft. Although I am rather amused at the idea of a theory concerning something I do in a completely untheoretical way, I am nonetheless pleased at the attention it is getting from these serious minds. I can only think of Julio Cortázar's instructive essay on how to ascend a staircase. Or is it descend? My intellectual attitudes toward this and other artistic matters have led me to be placed in the company of those of us called dinosaurs. I am really rather proud to bear the title. The dinosaur was an impressively large creature who therefore could only be sure of himself in his solitary solemnity. His stature enabled him to see far and wide and there were few barriers in his path. Rivers were as creeks to him. He was unassailable except by certain compeers. Those who call us dinosaurs must in turn receive an epithet which befits their activities and attitudes and compares them in a like way to some species of fauna. I opt for the hyena. He is a rather ungainly and awkward creature who travels in packs and lives off the carrion of prey brought down by nobler beasts. His call is a cacophony of sounds that is neither a roar nor a song and has been likened by many to a laugh. Also, in the spirit of postmodernist uncertainty, he is an ambiguous thing, looking somewhat like an ill-conceived dog but in truth (if I may use that word) more closely related to the cat, partaking neither of the sterling loyalty of the first nor the sensuous allure of the second.

It was while pondering such disquisitions that I struck upon the realization that my coevals and I are fourth-dimensional immigrants. We are of this land but not of this age. Our way has been a migration from our native time to this moment as we go dwindling down. I am a native of a period made up of three decades, much like the ones spoken of by Ortega y Gasset. These are the years when a person becomes himself. The years before were germination, those following, the melting icing on an already baked cake. My formation took shape in the thirties, the forties, and the fifties, a fearsome triad of decades which did indeed call for brontosaurian efforts at survival and sanity. Since spatial homelands have their sacred names and anthems, or should, I suggest that in the spirit of Rufus T. Firefly we sing "Hail, Hail, Brontosauria!" I leave the naming of subsequent epochs to the inhabitants thereof. Although we might consider "the Age of Similitude," since every other word used seems to be "like."

PART TWO

THE BILL OF PARTICULARS

THE BILL OF PARTICULARS

EXCLUDING SHORTER PIECES I have done, stories, essays, an occasional poem, the writers I have translated thus far number twenty-seven, with some awaiting publication and others for the propitious and appropriate moment when I can get to them. The works are largely fiction, with one small poetry chapbook, a literary study, and a social history. This varying array of personalities, styles, languages (Portuguese and Spanish), and nationalities all funneled into the work of one translator reveals how this last must in some way undergo a kind of controlled schizophrenia as he marshals his skills at mutability. My own experience in this matter has not been all that complex or worrisome. As I have said before, I follow the text, I let it lead me along, and a different and it is to be hoped proper style will emerge for each author. This bears out my thesis that a good translation is essentially a good reading; if we know how to read as we should we will be able to put down what we are reading in another language into our own. I might have said into our own words, but these, even in English, belong to the author who indirectly thought them up.

What follows will be my rap sheet, a consideration of my experience with the authors I have translated and, most especially, with their work. In some cases the work has been multiple, in others only a single book. My contacts have been personal with some, by correspondence with others, and in the cases of Machado de Assis and Vinícius de Moraes regretfully only through their work, although I do have some recordings of Vinícius reciting his poetry and singing his lyrics in a way that would have made Sinatra envious.

JULIO CORTÁZAR

Hopscotch (*Rayuela*, 1963). New York: Pantheon, 1966.

62: A Model Kit (*62: Modelo para armar*, 1968). New York: Pantheon, 1972.

A Manual for Manuel (*Libro de Manuel*, 1973). New York: Pantheon, 1978.

A Change of Light and Other Stories (*Octaedro*, 1974; *Alguien que anda por ahí*, 1978). New York: Knopf, 1980.

We Love Glenda So Much and Other Tales (*Queremos tanto a Glenda y otros relatos*, 1981). New York: Knopf, 1983.

A Certain Lucas (*Un tal Lucas*, 1979). New York: Knopf, 1984.

HOPSCOTCH WAS THE BOOK that got me started in translation, that won me that National Book Award, and also led me to do *One Hundred Years of Solitude*. García Márquez wanted me to do his book but at the moment I was tied up with Miguel Ángel Asturias's "banana trilogy." Cortázar told Gabo to wait, which he did, to the evident satisfaction of all concerned. So *Hopscotch* was for me what the hydrographic cliché calls a watershed moment as my life took the direction it was to follow from then on. I hadn't read the book but I skimmed some pages and did two sample chapters, the first and one farther along, I can't remember which. Editor Sara Blackburn and Julio both liked my version and I was off and away.

What drew me to the novel and to Julio were the variegated interests he and I had in common: jazz, humor, liberal politics, and inventive art and writing. As I have said, I read the complete novel only as I translated it. This strange and uncom-

mon procedure somehow followed the nature of the book itself and I do not think it hurt the translation in any way. Indeed, it may have insured its success. Cortázar had divided his
book into three sections: "From the Other Side," "From This
Side," and "From Diverse Sides," the last subtitled "Expendable
Chapters." He gives instructions on how to read the novel,
saying that it consists of many books, but two above all. We can
read it straight through, but stopping at the end of the second
section without continuing into the third. Then he lays out a
table for a second reading in which chapters from all three
sections are co-mingled in a different order. Each chapter in
this system has the number of the next chapter to be read at its
end. The last chapter, however, 131, tells you to go to 58, which
you have just read and were told to proceed to 131, so that by
this scheme you end up with a broken-record effect, where
the needle keeps jumping back and repeating and the song
never ends. Read this way the novel never ends, while if read
the first and seemingly proper way it does, saying ". . . let
himself go, paff, the end," implying that Oliveira, the protagonist, has defenestrated himself.

One stiff-necked critic was outraged that he should be
called upon to read the novel twice. Julio wrote me and figuratively shook his head over the fact that the poor boob did
not know that he was being toyed with. He went on to say
that it was bad enough to ask people to read his novel once, let
alone twice. He would never do such a thing. When I finished
the translation I remembered the instructions at the beginning
and realized that I had offered a third reading of the novel by
simply barging through from the first page to the last. What
that obtuse critic had not realized was that hopscotch is a
game, something to be played. The version that Julio had
sketched out on the cover of the novel was evidently the way

the game is played in Argentina, starting on a square called Earth and following the numbers to a square called Heaven. It was only natural that his intellectual friskiness should have been noticed by his countryman, Jorge Luis Borges, who was the first to publish Julio's work. Would that their poor, troubled, and so often solemn birthplace had been more like them in its history. Cortázar also maintained that our species was misnamed and should have been called *homo ludens* (nothing to do with any coughing gays).

In translating *Hopscotch* I think I was well served by my instinctive way of letting the words lead me. I say this because I did manage to get the drift of what the various and varied chapters were saying. Julio always matched his characters with their dialogues and monologues. He was quite keen in his awareness that the same person is apt to have a different style of speaking when talking to someone else then when talking to himself. Some primitive societies manage such discrepancies by a variety of case endings if not completely different lexicons. With Cortázar one has to be quickly aware of these twisty little tricks of expression that he's apt to pull. In one chapter Julio has Oliveira, his sometime narrator and some say his alter ego, glance at a book he has picked up in La Maga's room. The first line is strangely alien to both the period of the action and the style of the novel we are reading. But the second line says "And the things she reads, a clumsy novel . . ." and we realize that Cortázar is alternating, line by line, what Oliveira is thinking and what he is reading in her novel by Benito Pérez Galdós. I had to tread very carefully through this part so as not to let Oliveira's words influence those of Galdós and vice-versa.

This admixture is matched many times by the inclusion of such things as official documents from UNESCO, where

Cortázar worked as a translator himself. This last fact, instead of making me quiver with insecurity under the scrutiny of a master of the trade, relaxed me instead with the knowledge that Julio knew from experience what I was up against. Indeed, in some cases he would make suggestions that only a translator could make. So when I came to the documentation that he used to spice up the novel I found myself doing what he was doing for a living, faithfully translating the reports and resisting the temptation to make them conform a little. In one case there was no need for concern; he had devised a haiku made up of a list of Burmese names that he must have come across in some report or other.

As the first part of *Hopscotch* and some of the "Expendable Chapters" take place in Paris, quite a bit of French is woven into the narration. This could have been translated, but I left it as it was. Had Julio wanted these spots in English he would have translated them into Spanish in the first place. I also saw no reason to dumb the book down for readers of English and insult them in that way. I also left the Spanish intact sometimes for other reasons. Like any song, tangos are better left in the original or great and sometimes hilarious damage is done. I remember my opera-loving father's chuckling over the absurdity of translation in opera as he cited a recitative he had heard in a performance sung in English instead of Italian that went "Here comes the woman with the milk." The effect is the same as the one I mentioned somewhere when Mr. Smith replaced Mr. Bean at Merrill Lynch, which could have been the reason for James Merrill's abandoning the family trade.

It's hard enough to figure out what to do with languages other than the author's or the translator's, but what does one do with an invented one? Cortázar has one such tongue in *Hopscotch*. It's a language of love in that it describes amorous activity. It really isn't necessary to understand the words. The way they're strung together tells us what's going on. Their sound is suggestively helpful too. It is like Góngora's seemingly arcane poetry. I have found that knowing in detail what he's on about calls for exegesis and the death of his poetry. A simple reading aloud renders a feeling of what he is saying, much like the meaning we extract from a piece of music without knowing which notes are what. We can read Mallarmé's poem or listen to Debussy's prelude and the effect should be the same. This is how we approach Julio's *glíglico*. I had to translate it, however, so I put it into Gliglish rather than English and I think I kept enough of its substance to make even Mr. Frost happy, but I wasn't out to please him, only my readers and perhaps Mr. Joyce.

I was aided in this venture by having listened to all manner of phrases from a language called Vermacian, put together by my daughter Clara at an early age to be spoken to her Snoopy doll. It was just foolish enough to match the foolish nature with which she had endowed him. Like Gliglish, it has an English base, which would lead some to call it a dialect. Snoopy would simply say of himself that he had a "speech defeck," not such an acceptable term today, better left in Vermacian. For some mysterious reason it veers toward the Slavic in its endings, with genitive-sounding things like Snoopev, Momev, and Dadev. This has defied explanation on everyone's part and calls for the expertise of a psycho-linguist. Clara had met Julio and was impressed with his height, comparing him to President Lincoln and calling him "the six-foot-four man." In his correspondence there would always be a sketch for her. As can be seen from some of his stories, there is some kind of bond between Cortázar and small children, a mutual recognition and understanding that goes beyond notation. In so many ways he was a great child, large and pure, and children can sense those who are their peers, even when they look them over coldly as one dog does another.

As I see it from here, Cortázar has threaded a great deal of his work into what could be the woof and warp of a kind of tapestry. This thought emerges after all has been said and done, if ever done it is. I can see this in the second of his novels that I translated, *62: A Model Kit*. My title is quite close to his, *62: Modelo para armar*, a model to be assembled. This last is much too awkward and all it does is describe what is commonly called a model kit (in my day it would have been an Erector Set or a less realistic Tinker Toy). The 62 in the title refers to Chapter 62 in *Hopscotch* where Julio's Pessoa-like near heteronym, the writer Morelli, explains how he would write a novel. Morelli provides the elements and Cortázar fastens them together for his novel. In a certain way this novel could be called a dream version of *Hopscotch*, a surrealist dream perhaps, but, then, all dreams are surrealist and hence the source of magic realism. It might be called an ephemeral version of the earlier book so I was faced with translating something that had already been translated, albeit inside one of those mysterious extra dimensions physicists talk about. The oddballs of *Hopscotch* here become true weirdlings.

The narration starts in the first person and then changes to the third and names the protagonist narrator as Juan. At other times this protagonist/witness is someone referred to as *mi paredro*. The best I could do in tracking this down was to come up with the Greek *paredros*, which is evidently the Hellenized version of some sort of ancient Egyptian *Doppelgänger*. Faced with this cross-cultural mélange, I opted for the Greek instead of searching out the scroll of Thoth because the name of that worthy sounds true only in the mouth of Boris Karloff. There can be a problem in the fact that the Spanish is stressed on the second syllable, paredro, while the Anglo-Greek comes on a paredros. The English reader, like his Spanish counterpart, is most likely left in the dark concerning all this, which is in the spirit of the story.

Cortázar has invented two classically ludicrous characters here, Polanco and Calac, who will burst into dialogue in some strange tongue of their own which at times is shared by others. It is much like the Gliglish of *Hopscotch* and I saw fit to handle it in the same way, preserving the root and anglicizing the endings. For example, Calac and Polanco continually swap insults, the one calling the other a *petiforro* and being called a *cronco* in return. These I rendered as *pettifor* and *cronk* and they seem to maintain their tone of meaningless denigration in the flow of the English prose. It may be meaningless to the uninitiate, but one who has worked on Cortázar in both English and Spanish will not have much of a problem in extracting the juice of their intent.

It is along these lines that I try to feel out the definition of the person Julio calls a *cronopio*. The meaning of this really untranslatable designation can only be essayed by saying that it stands for a person endowed with that equally untranslatable Brazilian quality called *jeito*. He is a person who may be the only one who can fix a machine one day and then throw in the proverbial monkey wrench the next. I thought of Cronos and chronology and time, but Julio said it has nothing to do with that. He said that a person knows if he is a cronopio simply by being one, no explanation needed, *jeito* or *jeitinho* at work. It is my great honor to have been dubbed cronopio by Julio Cortázar and I bear the title with the pride of a knight, comrade in arms of the Knight of the Woeful Countenance. The idea of the cronopio has much to do with how I translate

Julio. I sometimes think that while I was doing his stuff I my-self was his paredros, doing what he had done in a different time and place. I like to think that I still am.

I did a few other books by Julio, short stories, sketches, and another novel. This last is rather different from the ones we have been considering. Cortázar wrote it at the start of the military dictatorship in Argentina, as the tin-plate generals went about their pathological war of attrition against the young and the forlorn with no fear of any opposition from tanks or trained infantry (the British would teach them later what war was really like). As un-Argentine as Julio has looked to his shallow-minded accusers (born in Belgium, living in Paris), he felt more Argentine than any of that pack and, like Borges under similar accusation, proved it with his writ-ings. In order to present a picture of the expatriate opposition, Cortázar wrote his *Libro de Manuel* (Manuel's Book or Book of Manuel). The possible titles in English were troublesome for us, too bland or too biblical. We finally settled on my own hesitant suggestion of *A Manual for Manuel*. I still wonder if we might not have done better, perhaps in this case a title a little more far-removed from the original. Julio, ever the cronopio, however, was intrigued by the play on words, even though he could have done the same in Spanish but hadn't. For some rea-son related to all this perhaps, *Manual* doesn't seem to rollick as much as the other novels, although there is one fine scene of a turquoise penguin ambling along the streets of Paris on its way back to Antarctica. Maybe it's because Calac and Polanco aren't there to set the tone or perhaps it's because the dictator-ship hovering over the book is not a fit matter for Julio's humor. Black as it can be, it might just not be apt for that grim Argentine reality so close to his heart. García Márquez and Demetrio Aguilera-Malta could have had what we might call "fun" with brutal dictators, but Cortázar is evidently on a different bent; his inner child perhaps.

I did quite a few of Julio's stories and found that they adapted rather well to English. That weary old debate over the term "magic realism" gets livened up when Cortázar's stories are considered. In so many cases we have the smooth metamorphosis of what we deem reality into something that's really there but shouldn't be according to our lights. Sometimes an inexplicable act or object is defined by an equally inexplicable word. The mystery lies in the fact that an object can be inexplicable and yet exist in front of our eyes. We can go into a dream like Sor Juana Inés de la Cruz as she sought after her own "theory of everything" or we can bring it into our own existence by giving it a name, a word. Is an object described in Gliglish any less real than when described in English or Spanish? In moments like these the translator must delve after the writer's genius, as Harold Bloom does, and try to fit it into his own, become a true paredros. I found that while I would have to belabor my wits to solve such problems with Miguel Ángel Asturias and other writers, with Julio Cortázar the blend was smooth.

The last book by Cortázar that I translated was *A Certain Lucas*. As I look back there is a saddening or maybe a gladdening moment when I realize that the translation came out in 1984, the year Julio died. There must be something deeper and more mysterious to all this because I feel that of all his books this is the most Julio one. This Lucas has to be his paredros or whatever he would have called him at the time. The idea of the double is described in one of his essayistic pieces put in between two batches of Lucas, wherein he notes that Dr. Jekyll knew about Mr. Hyde but that Hyde didn't know about Jekyll. In some odd way this might be applied to the author-translator relationship in reverse order. As the author (Jekyll) writes his words he doesn't know at the time that the translator (Hyde) is to take over in a sense and become the author as he transforms the text. Let us hope that the outcome will be happier than it was for Stevenson's hero and his paredros.

I have explained above how I began my work as a professional translator with *Hopscotch* and how I found that Julio and I had so many notions in common. This must have aided my translation because in all the subsequent things of his I did there was a kind of natural flow of expression that I only find when I am writing something personal without any restraints from matters like academic purposes. This flow would continue along through both standard and quirky turns of expression. My wife Clementine also essayed her hand at translating Julio. She did his story "Summer" from *A Change of Light and Other Stories*. Her approach and her views on translating are different from mine, as they should be. We never go over each other's work as critics would and instead, more often than not, offer voluntary suggestions that are apt to be joyfully accepted as they improve the work at hand. Out of this experience Clem brought her own novella entitled *Summer II*, quite different in intent but with some sort of mystic kinship if only obvious in the title. She also allows that Edith Wharton might have had a hand in it, although the story is really very Julio.

The idea I have broached that the translator must not sacrifice himself, must not betray himself by becoming someone else as he translates does not really run counter to what I have been saying above. This brings me to Miguel de Unamuno's notion that the *Quijote* and its knight were there all the time but that Cervantes just got there first. Unamuno never forgave his namesake, saying that he had really been meant to write the book. We can sense this in the way he wrote his novel, or *nivola* as he called it, *Niebla* (*Mist*), and it also might explain why there have been ever so many good translations of *Don Quixote* done over the years, each one Cervantes's creation and each one also the personal creation of the translator and therefore a fine piece of work, even when mutton is rendered into lamb.

It is my feeling that by having Julio Cortázar as my first author I was put into just the proper mood and mode for translating others to come. As I blended my words with his I must have slipped into the role of *paredros* and was doing in English what he had been doing in Spanish, largely unaware but somehow instinctively knowing. Hyde was getting to know Jekyll. They were beginning to resemble each other but could never become one another as they worked in different dimensions of language that could only produce reflections. I am not sure that I could have written *Hopscotch* had I got there first, but I did get it into an English version that Julio approved and liked as did some others. I wonder now in my ninth decade as I watch words fade and then glimmer back into new meanings and nuances if someone will be following me at some future time into a reproduction of what Julio wrote. It could go on and on, for translations have the strange progressive literary virtue of never being finished. If we have read *Hopscotch* properly we can see that it, too, was never really finished, that Cortázar is inviting us to do what he had not done. If that is to be the case, let us keep Avellaneda, whoever he was, in mind as he tried to finish Cervantes's work but left us with an amusing little tale that trips along to nowhere. As a matter of fact it ends up in the booby hatch, a place where Don Quixote wouldn't be caught dead (and wasn't). The completion of a work is best done in translation, where the translator can work at things denied the author in his own language, even the way Saint Jerome mistakenly implied the cuckoldry of Moses which Michelangelo then wrought in enduring stone. To carry this to a fittingly inconclusive conclusion, I suggest that in the sense or nonsense of it, every translation I have done since *Hopscotch* has in some way or another been its continuation.

Mulata (*Mulata de tal*, 1963). New York: Delacorte, 1967.
Strong Wind (*Viento fuerte*, 1950). New York: Delacorte, 1969.
The Green Pope (*El papa verde*, 1954). New York: Delacorte, 1971.
The Eyes of the Interred (*Los ojos de los enterrados*, 1960). New York: Delacorte, 1973.

I SHALL GO ABOUT REMEMBERING the authors I have translated in some sort of chronological order. I do this because I know that each work I did influenced the next in some way. Despite the fact that my first big job, *Hopscotch*, was well received does not mean that I wouldn't be learning all manner of techniques, so-called, and approaches, also so-called, in the process of translation. Learning by doing, as they say in kindergarten, is how my skills must have increased as I've gone along, but there was always the peril of settling down into some comfortable calcified position from which to await oncoming assignments. I think it was the variety of authors and books I encountered that kept my mind loose and probing. There is always the danger, however, of translating Peter the way I translate Paul. I think that my amateurish probes saved me from this. I leave strategy to the theorists as I confine myself to tactics. Habit and dogma do have their place, however, and can bring about unsuspected benefits. High-school dramatics in the Footlighters with Miss Edmonds certainly helped give me a sense of how to handle other people's speech, just as I like to think that having been reared as a papist in my early years was responsible for my scoring highest on the rifle range with the M-1 during basic from the kneeling position because of all those years of genuflections, although both those experiences may have been responsible in bringing on a touch of arthritis in those joints.

Soon after doing *Hopscotch* I was approached by Seymour Lawrence, who had inaugurated his own imprint under the aegis of Delacorte Press, to consider doing something by the Guatemalan novelist-folklorist Miguel Ángel Asturias. His best-known novel, *El Señor Presidente*, which dealt with dictatorship, had already appeared in English and had been well received for its grim dark atmosphere of tyranny. I had wondered why they had not translated the title but came to see that *Mr. President* would have had too much the ring of the White House about it. Sam Lawrence and I discussed matters and agreed on doing Asturias's strange and surreal novel (magic surrealism?) *Mulata de tal*, my favorite among his works. The title presented us with a terrible problem for translation. The term means a Mulatto woman of rather doubtful reputation, devoid of respect. If she were addressed that way it could be translated as "You goddamned Mulatto wench." It might also mean any old Mulatto woman. The same *tal* as used in Cortázar's *Un tal Lucas* precedes the noun and therefore means *A Certain Lucas*, as the book was titled in English. The French translation of *Mulata* which had already come out called it *Une Certaine Mulatresse*, conveying a more benevolent tone. Sam and I pondered and debated and finally decided to call the book simply *Mulata*, keeping the Spanish word and avoiding any rigorous and impossible effort to deal with the *tal*. When the book came out in England, however, the publishers called it *The Mulatta and Mr. Fly*. I wasn't so sure about that. *Mulatta* here is a bastardized word, the feminine ending has no place in English and could only be valid in Italy, where the word originated, a far piece from the jungles of Guatemala. As for Mr. Fly, that epithet refers to the opening on a pair of trousers and has nothing to do with the insect. Celestino Yumí, the protagonist, is called *Brujo Bragueta*, or as I put it the Fly Wizard because of his penchant for going into church with his fly open in order to tempt women receiving communion into mortal sin. When I first saw "Mr. Fly" my mind immediately went back and picked up on June Christie's lyrics in Stan Kenton's "Across the Alley from the Alamo." As can be seen from all this the business of titles in translation leads to many impossibilities as well as any number of infelicitous attempts. My wife Clementine and I once took part in a panel on just this subject. If Sam and I had done a complete change in title we would have been better off with something other than the British version, but the idea of *mulata* would have been sacrificed.

Shortly after publication Asturias was awarded the Nobel Prize for literature. There was the usual outcry from chauvinistic critics whenever the prize goes to an author known only to the Swedish Academy. It could be argued that it had been due to the Swedes' sometimes evident geopolitical motivations and that Asturias was less deserving than some of his Latin American contemporaries, but *Mulata* especially is what Lévi-Strauss might have called the raw meat of magic realism before authors who were better literary gourmets began to cook it up. We must remember that Asturias had started out in the dismal science but abandoned economics to go into anthropology and that his novels ended up there even when the theme was political. They must have been aware of this in Sweden. I like to think that *Mulata* might have pushed them across. Sam Lawrence's immediate reaction was to redo the dust jacket, replacing one that I thought set the tone admirably, with a more sedate and less inviting one trumpeting his winning of the prize.

The tempo of the book is frenetic and I had to be sure that I wasn't using any "slow" words. For this I had to rely on instinct, natural-born or acquired, and as I normally do I simply followed the words once more. This was not always that easy as the tale is embedded in folklore and religion as Satan, known as Candanga, brought over by the Spaniards along with their cross, moves about among the ancient Mayan deities who would squash him, and a poor Catholic priest is assailed from both sides. The Devil urges people to breed so he can collect more souls for Hell. Satan, too, is against birth control. The going was hard for me at times as I sought out persuasive equivalents for so many local names that also carried some meaning, either in Maya-Quiché or in the bastardized Spanish spoken by the peasantry. At times I would have to invent new portmanteau words, trespassing into the eloquent world of *Finnegans Wake*.

After *Mulata*, with some reservations, I undertook the patently political novels of the so-called banana trilogy, which dealt with the domination of Central America's politics and economy by the United Fruit Company. My doubts came from the fact that Latin American publishing in those days was in woeful need of good editing, something along the lines of Maxwell Perkins's paring down the writings of Thomas Wolfe to the manageable size of a good novel. These three books by Asturias, getting fatter and fatter as they went along, needed trimming, if not down to the dimensions of a haiku at least to the proportions of one long novel. Editing might also have eliminated some of the author's misconceptions of North American society, as half the main characters are from the States. Here I had to restrain myself as much as I could, maintaining as always my belief that translators are not in the silk-purse business. Every so often I did have to intervene, however, as was the case with a character called Geo Maker Thompson. I thought about this for some time. Has Asturias mistaken the old and honored abbreviation Geo. (whatever happened to this and those other delightful ones, Jas., Chas., and Thos.?) for a given name? Or had he thought it was the way Joe was written, as no period followed? I decided that it was a case of the former and went for George in its entirety, figuring that Geo would have been too offputting for a reader in English. It also seems that he thought Maker Thompson was the usual Spanish combination of paternal and maternal surnames in that order. A lack of concern for foreign names shows up in other writers I have done and there, too, I have made what I considered the necessary corrections, albeit judiciously. We must remember, however, that writers in English too often are befuddled by the word order of surnames in Spanish and Portuguese.

These three novels, *Strong Wind, The Green Pope,* and *The Eyes of the Interred* (I made *enterrados* interred for reasons of euphony, *buried* would have been a clinker here), are really more folkloric than magical. They offered occasional problems with localized parlance and exotic flora and fauna and I searched the lexicon of botanical and other names from the British West Indies as they were once called, because a similar climate would support the same species. I was not always successful, however, and came to appreciate the advantage of English usage where the word *tree* can follow whatever mysterious name is used in Spanish or Mayan to designate the plant. Once when I had come upon a troublesome tree in *Mulata*, whose English name I found nowhere, I decided to consult the extant French translation for help. Alas, lacking the convenient out we have in English my poor Gallic counterpart had the man sitting under a simple *arbre*, nothing more.

As can be seen from all of the above, I was not entirely satisfied with my handling of the novels of Asturias. The wild *Walpurgisnacht* of *Mulata* gave me a lot of fun at its making, but maybe, like Edmund of Gloucester, the result was a bastard. I like to think it wasn't. As for the trilogy, about which I had my doubts at the start, when I peruse it now it doesn't seem too bad at all, quite up to the limits of my possibilities. Maybe my casual lack of system, flying by the seat of my pants, as it were, was the best way to approach texts not entirely to my liking. I still remember how Quentin Anderson described those of us teaching Humanities A (the Great Books) with him at Columbia as "brilliant amateurs." I also remember that those of us amateurs in the OSS left at war's end to pursue what we were meant to do, if ever that was so, and we left behind our clerkish comrades to go ahead and found the CIA, with all of its consequent intelligence blunders and blasphemies as they call themselves a "community," as though they were Cistercian monks or something. I continue to feel comfortable as an amateur and a dilettante, it makes life freer and more friendly for me.

I never met Asturias although I did have a bit of warm correspondence with him. I still try to defend his work (and Nobel Prize) from attacks that might sometimes be justified behind the malice and I shall always defend him from his detractors because of the many brave positions he took during his life and for his attempts to explain the sadly never-resolved state of his miscegenated country with great whirls of fancy, difficult to understand but eloquent and revealing when there's just a grain of vision there.

CLARICE LISPECTOR

The Apple in the Dark (*A Maçã no Escuro*, 1961). New York: Knopf, 1967.

WHEN I FIRST GOT TO Brazil in 1962 the books people were talking about were two novels: *Grande Sertão: Veredas*, by João Guimarães Rosa (translated as *The Devil to Pay in the Backlands*, ugh!) and *The Apple in the Dark*, by Clarice Lispector. I got hold of them at once and was pleased to see how two different writers could handle the theme of life's bewilderment in its Brazilian context with such contrasting styles and with such diverging characters and come to the same inconclusion, one befitting their time and country. A few years later I met Clarice at a conference on Brazil in Texas where she was the featured speaker. I was flabbergasted to meet that rare person who looked like Marlene Dietrich and wrote like Virginia Woolf. She also had those *Kyrgizenaugen* that so fascinated Thomas Mann. Back in New York I was invited to lunch by Alfred Knopf to talk about Brazilian books. He had recently been married in Rio de Janeiro and this had increased his warm feelings for the country and his interest in its writers. He had already published books by Gilberto Freyre and wanted to do some more things, including Clarice's book. *Hopscotch* was behind me and I was finishing *Mulata*, so I was ready to take on another job. The conditions were ideal because I was preparing to leave for Brazil on my Fulbright and Clarice would be available in case I needed any help.

This was to be my first translation from the Portuguese and my being in Brazil was a great help in catching on to the vernacular of the place. Having studied, read, and spoken a lot of Spanish until then, I had to be careful not to miss the differing meanings of so many cognates common to the sister tongues. When I had first begun to learn Portuguese the Spanish would interfere, but on my return from Brazil it was quite the other way around and I found I now had trouble teaching or speaking Spanish as I labored to keep the Portuguese at bay. At risk of offending or dismaying my many friends who speak Spanish, I must admit here and now that I prefer Portuguese, especially in the Brazilian oral mode with all its unique sounds and rhythms. Some of the sounds, like the open O and the dark L, are closer to Slavic noises than to those of other Romance languages. This breadth makes for all kinds of varying styles and this can be seen in the two novels I have mentioned above. I was glad to be translating *The Apple in the Dark* and not *Grande Sertão: Veredas*. Clarice goes smoothly into English, Rosa would have to be rewritten, not translated, unless by the likes of James Joyce. His translator is immediately faced with an impossibility: Rosa's epigraph reads *O diabo na rua no meio do redemoinho* (The devil in the street in the middle of the whirlwind). Take a good look at the word for whirlwind: *redemoinho*. There sandwiched in is the word *demo*, so that the devil is not only in the middle of the whirlwind but is in the middle of the word for it. The novel had already been translated but a lot had been slurred over and a lot had been left out. When Emir Rodríguez Monegal and Thomas Colchie were putting together their *Borzoi Anthology of Latin American*

Literature they both agreed on the chunk of *Grande Sertão* that would give the best sense of the book as a whole. Since a good part of their anthology made use of extant translations they went to *The Devil to Pay in the Backlands* and found that their sought-after selection had been one of the many parts left out. Tom Colchie had to do his own translation, which stands out when held against the purported version.

I think that the discrepancies between Spanish and Portuguese should be as evident in their translation as in the original languages. Wishful thinking though it may be, I like to imagine that one can sense in some mysterious way the language from which a text has been translated without its being ruinous to the English version. A test I propose is the reading of a translation in English with an accent, the way it would sound if read by a native speaker (that term always brings on the image of a Fiji islander speaking pidgin to mind), one whose English is not completely fluent soundwise. Petch Peden has caught the *mexicanidad* of Juan Rulfo's *Pedro Páramo* so perfectly that if you heard it read by Alfonso Bedoya ("I don't need no stinkin' batch") you'd think you were listening to the original Spanish. My Portuguese is Brazilian and my Spanish is a kind of general American Spanish but when I am doing a book I try to hear the accent of the speaker's country. From the Argentine I hear *cabazho* for *caballo* and from a Cuban I hear *ehuela* for *escuela*. The Portuguese from Portugal may look the same as its Brazilian counterpart, but it can sound altogether different. The Portuguese contract their sounds to make them fit into their small country while the Brazilians expand theirs to make them fit into their huge land. Any Mexican going to Buenos Aires can make his way quite well, but I have heard of Brazilians who speak English when they go to Lisbon because they would have trouble understanding their native language as it is spoken there. A favorite Brazilian word of mine is the one for ignition, *ignicão*. Not only do Brazilians add a vowel but they go ahead and stress it, ee-gee'-nee-são.

Most of this didn't enter in as I went about translating *The Apple in the Dark*. Clarice Lispector writes a clear, flowing, and evocative prose. A translator following her words should be led right along by them and have no trouble. As we entered the age of assorted chauvinisms I was continually asked if I had found any problems in translating a female author. I was never sure how to answer that. I have subsequently translated the work of other women and as I think about it I was always more concerned with the style than with the sex of the writer. What people call sexual politics did raise its head during the making of the translation, however. I heard that the editor at Knopf was outraged at the audacity of a female writer to have a male protagonist (actually, the two women involved in the story could be said to share that role to a large extent). I wondered why he wasn't upset that I, a male, dared to translate a novel written by a female author, and shouldn't like recrimination have been directed at Tolstoy and Flaubert among so many others?

Clarice subsequently turned out several more fine novels and stories but I didn't do them. Her story "The Crime of the Mathematics Professor" had appeared in *Odyssey* as we went about discovering new talent. There was no breakup of any kind, just the usual situation in which I was working on something else. There was, however, what might be called a proxy situation as two of my best students at the CUNY Graduate School, Elizabeth Lowe and Earl Fitz, went on to translate some Clarice with great success. The beautiful Clarice Lispector was not treated well by life. Betrayed in marriage, her lovely face was severely burned in a fire in her apartment in Leme, Rio de Janeiro. The deep-feeling Clarice went on to suffer a terribly painful illness and death at much too early an age. As John Kennedy is said to have remarked, "Life isn't fair."

Knopf asked me to write an introduction to the novel because they felt that it would be difficult to understand. I disagreed but was glad to oblige. Afterwards I wondered if it really was needed or whether the novel was more arcane than I had thought. In that case my explication would probably only be one of many possible twists. This bears out my idea that every reader reads his or her own book. One nice bit about *The Apple in the Dark* is that Alfred Knopf saw to it that the translator's name appeared on the dust jacket. This was a recognition that would be long in coming with other publishers and after Alfred went upstairs Knopf was lax in following it up.

MARIO VARGAS LLOSA

The Green House (*La casa verde*, 1965). New York: Harper &
   Row, 1968.
Conversation in The Cathedral (*Conversación en la Catedral*, 1969).
   New York: Harper & Row, 1975.

BACK IN THE LATE SIXTIES the organization most responsible
for the dissemination in the United States of the works of the
Latin American "Boom" was the Center for Inter-American
Relations on Park Avenue, since absorbed into the Americas
Society. The moving spirit in the literary sphere of the Center
was the Venezuelan sculptor José Guillermo Castillo. He was a
charmer who was quite adept at gentle arm-twisting to get
someone to take on a translation and then covering the publisher's costs for it. I remember the night when he and Cass
Canfield, Jr., worked on me and cajoled me into doing a new
novel by the Peruvian writer Mario Vargas Llosa, who had
been dissatisfied with how his work had been translated before. As it turned out, I was not upset with my agreement to
do so. The book was *The Green House*, which, once again, I had
not read. On hearing the title one might assume offhand,
thinking it was one word, that it had to do with florists. This
was not the case. The house was of the kind called bawdy and
the word *verde* in Spanish has off-color connotations, some-

thing impossible to maintain literally in English translation. But then, too, the name could be applied to the Amazon jungle (impossible to use rain forest as a euphemism here), where the story has its start and finish. When I learned that I immediately thought of W. H. Hudson's *Green Mansions*, but soon found that there was no romantic idealization here. The book really consists of two novels, or two aspects of the same one, that could stand as different tales, one that starts in the jungle but is transmogrified into the second that takes place in the desert city of Piura in northern Peru. Many of the characters are the same but their names and stations have undergone alteration.

Some of the names offered difficulty in translation. The best I could do with a blond soldier called *El Rubio* was to make him Blondy. Someone remarked that Whitey would have been better, but at the time Black Panthers were active and the connotations would have been otherwise, and the soldier in question was obviously not a full member of what has been called the white race. There might also have been a problem with gender and the old comic-strip character, but she spelled her name Blondie, although I may have been thinking of a baseball player somewhere in the past called Blondy Ryan. And there was also Hitler's dog. Towhead was out, too rustic American.

As in the novels of Asturias there was the matter of flora and fauna. Things worked out better here. If my Spanish dictionary failed me I would consult the one in Portuguese, which also covers the Amazon basin. This is the wonderful *Nôvo Aurélio*, compiled by Aurélio Buarque de Holanda (Chico Buarque's uncle), which Nélida Piñon had given me. Lately, however, I have found that it has left me high and dry regarding certain words from the area that lies between Brazil and French Guiana as I translate the novel *Saraminda*, by José Sarney, former president of Brazil and a fine novelist. Now a senator from the state of Amapá, he probably has had more jungle experience than either Mario or Aurélio Buarque de Holanda.

There is an extremely fascinating character in *The Green House*, the Japanese-Brazilian smuggler and badman Fushía, who runs his sector of the jungle with a cruel and iron hand. Years after the novel was written Vargas Llosa went into politics and ran for president of Peru. Like so many young liberals in Latin America (and elsewhere), with the years he has drifted rightward and was the candidate of the oligarchical upper class that has run things there whenever the army has allowed them to. The country was in a chaotic state and Mario's populist opponent, the Japanese-Peruvian Alberto Fujimori, promised everything and trounced him. He went on to betray the people's hopes and backslid into the usual corrupt dictatorship. My immediate thought was that here was Fushía wreaking his revenge on Mario for having created him as such a baleful figure in the novel.

With this novel Vargas Llosa became one of that group practicing what would be called, for better or for worse, magic realism. I found him closer to Asturias than to Cortázar, but that could have been due to a similarity in terrain. There is nothing otherworldly in *The Green House*, although the characters, this-worldly as they are, have the proportions of monsters and, also, the atmosphere of the story is overloaded with tension, and tension is the stuff of magic. Given all this, I had to tread carefully, not choosing words that would be completely magical in tone or picking ones that would be too drably realistic. The original helped in this because Mario had just the right words and if I sensed and chose the right English ones I was home.

Mario looked over my work as I went along and would offer suggestions. Most were appreciated, especially where it had been some jungle peculiarity I had missed. At times, however, he would latch on to what he thought was a mistake and offer a correction. His limited English had simply kept him unaware of the fact that my word was nothing but a synonym for the one he was suggesting. He was wary of the novel's becoming too exotic in tone and I had to tell him that it would be hard for a North American not to find exotic even the most banal aspects of Amazonian existence and that if the translation was to be true there was little that could be done to offset that impression. I also reminded him that the Spanish reader in Madrid, or even in Lima, would find it no less so. Here was a case of magic realism by definition, as what was real in Iquitos would come off as something magical in northern climes. I am sure that if Fushía could have read the book as his biography he would have found nothing unreal about his surroundings or even, perhaps, about his own strange self.

A few years later Cass Canfield came back with another Vargas Llosa novel to be translated: *Conversación en la Catedral* (*Conversation in The Cathedral*). You will note that *Catedral* is capitalized in Spanish and that both *Cathedral* and the article are in English. This is because the locale in question is not the cathedral of Lima at all but a bar across the way that takes its name from it. This made for great trouble in maintaining the capitalized article in reviews and notices, given the fact that no one was aware of that circumstance without having read the book. I have always tried to hew as closely as possible to the title of the book I am translating and we have seen that it has worked out thus far. I think it is disrespectful in a certain way to mess around and take extreme liberties with a book's title. I was pleased that when I was asked to translate two of Machado de Assis's masterpieces I was able to rescue their titles from the absurdity that had befallen them in previous otherwise adequate translations: *The Posthumous Memoirs of Brás Cubas* from *Epitaph of a Small Winner* and *Quincas Borba* from *Philosopher or Dog?*. The reasoning behind such altered titles might have called *Madame Bovary* something like *Adultery and a Norman Doctor's Wife* and *Anna Karenina* could have been *The Lady and the Guardsman*.

Unlike *The Green House, Conversation* is patently political, although the underlying psychological and social aspects of life in a corrupt dictatorship are more important as they are reflected in the characters. The structure is complicated. The title refers to a meeting in the aforementioned bar between Santiago Zavala, son of an upper-class politician, and Ambrosio, the family's former chauffeur. This chat covers the near and more distant past of the family during the dictatorship of General Odría. Vargas Llosa has pulled off a temporal trick that will confuse the reader at first until he catches on to what's up. The conversation that starts the book is in the present tense as Zavala and Ambrosio begin to reminisce. Then time drifts into the past as they go back and what was past for the past then goes farther back to the pluperfect. This technique does a superb job of time travel back and forth but I had to be ever so careful to follow and not make any slips in tense, so as not to throw the story out of kilter and confuse the reader further.

The Spanish system of tenses, like in all the other Romance languages I know, includes two, sometimes three, past tenses, each with a definite temporal connotation. In English the distinctions are less specific. We were taught in Spanish A1 (I refer to pre-digital days when there were no computers and no Spanish 101) that *hablaba* was *was speaking* and *habló* was *spoke*. If we translate the first always in the progressive form, however, we can fall into an unnatural monotony as the sense of that particular action might be better served by *spoke*. Here the translator must act instinctively and read the English that lies behind the Spanish, not what the grammar book calls for, as he transforms the Spanish and describes the episode. This particular vicissitude can be the ruination of a simple line of poetry.

There was one important name or nickname that gave me trouble and I am not sure that I really solved the problem of its translation. The head of Odría's secret police in the novel and a key figure in the story is one Cayo Bermúdez, who took a perverted pleasure in calling himself Cayo Mierda. What was I to do with the "dirty word?" Plain old *shit* doesn't fit as a substitute surname. An individual can quite easily be called a shit in the predicate, as W. H. Auden is supposed to have done after reading the Book of Job and remarking, "Isn't God a shit?" But I needed something closer to a nickname. A euphemism of sorts like *turd* would not do for the same reasons and I would lose the impact of that fine old basic word with all its concomitant connotations. I finally decided upon Cayo Shithead, using a rather current epithet that goes better with a Christian name and is not too far from Auden's use of *shit*.

I have found that what used to be socially forbidden but is now acceptable speech can often be a problem in translation across cultures. *Hijo de puta* must be *son of a bitch* and not *whoreson*, which went out with the Elizabethans. Then there is also *cabrón*, meaning billy goat, but which has come to mean a deceived husband or lover, the opposite of that supposedly lustful horned creature. Try calling someone around here "cuckold" and be prepared for the dumb look you will get instead of the knife that would have been forthcoming in Mexico and other places, although *cabrón* has also lost some of its original nastiness and can also be rendered simply as *son of a bitch.*

As Mario shifted to the Right politically he fell out with former friends who had stayed true to their early positions. This was particularly true of his relationship with Gabriel García Márquez. Vargas Llosa's doctoral dissertation was an excellent study of the latter and was published as *García Márquez, historia de un deicidio* (the story of a deicide). Because of their quarrel Vargas Llosa has forbidden the translation of this book into English, thus depriving readers in that language of his insights regarding his fellow novelist.

Vargas Llosa has gone on to write several more novels, but I haven't done any of them, having been tied up as usual with other projects as the publishers looked elsewhere. I have no regrets on this score as I think I had the fun of doing his best work so far. In all truth I am glad that I did not have to translate his *War of the End of the World*, which is a fictionalized version of the story of Antônio Conselheiro, the Brazilian visionary, and his revolt in the back country of Bahia in Brazil. I cannot see how anyone can improve on the novelistic reportage of Euclides da Cunha in his *Os Sertões* (*Rebellion in the Backlands*). Any comparison always brings to mind Cervantes and Avellaneda.

AFRÂNIO COUTINHO

An Introduction to Literature in Brazil (Introdução à Literatura no Brasil, 1966). New York: Columbia University Press, 1969.

SOMEWHAT AGAINST MY BETTER judgment I agreed to translate a book of criticism, *An Introduction to Literature in Brazil*, by Afrânio Coutinho. I was used to translating fiction and an occasional poem. Although I had done critical articles, I had never done a full-length book. It turned out that I had been right in my doubts. Afrânio's book is intelligent, original, well-written, and worthwhile, but the language of criticism and critical theory offered few adventures and not a great deal of creativity for the translator. It got to be a rather boring job as I went at it. The word *introduction* really has a hidden double meaning here. It is, of course, just what it says, an introduction to literature in Brazil, giving it the touch of breadth implied therein, but this study first appeared as the introduction to an excellent multi-volumed collection of literary essays by various hands edited by Coutinho and called simply *A Literatura no Brasil* (Literature in Brazil). The title of the translation is somewhat deceptive therefore, although I saw no problem in maintaining it since it does cover the material inside.

I was fortunate that the postmodernist monster had not breached as yet, so I was spared the problem of any turgid and neo-arcane monstrosities to translate. Afrânio was of the now old school of New Criticism, of which I was a contemporary and therefore an adept, having studied Joyce, Hopkins, and Stevens among others with William York Tindall during my graduate student days at Columbia. As I have noted, Portuguese, and most especially the Brazilian variety, is eminently supple, matching English in this respect, unlike French and Spanish, and therefore it renders translation equally free and easy, less restricted. With Spanish I have to walk that narrow line between tight and loose structure, careful not to betray one language or the other. With Portuguese I can let myself go, in a manner of speaking, careful to avoid the other vicissitudes involved.

I had used the Coutinho collection of critical essays when I was teaching Brazilian literature and now I had a chance to go through the introduction properly, word for word, from start to finish. It was helpful in better organizing my knowledge as I plodded along. Also, this review of Brazilian literature, as well as many of its Portuguese antecedents, gave me a sense of the whole body, which is what Afrânio aims to do in his introduction. It also furnished me with the proper frame of mind to work on the Brazilian novels that awaited me.

Mention must be made of a picaresque episode that took place during Afrânio's coming to Columbia as visiting professor, which is how I came to translate the book for Columbia University Press. Charles Wagley, the anthropologist, had obtained a visiting professorship for Latin American scholars and writers. As the chair rotated among the various disciplines the time for literature had come around again. As a Brazilianist, Chuck Wagley was eager to get someone from Brazil and we immediately thought of Afrânio Coutinho, the most original and the wisest literary eminence of the moment. The last time the chair had been allotted to literature I had suggested the Nicaraguan poet and critic Ernesto Mejía Sánchez. He came to Columbia and gave some of the best courses ever given in the Department of Spanish and Portuguese. Ernesto subsequently became the ambassador to Spain for the new Sandinista government, but he died in Madrid at much too early an age. Mejía Sánchez's training came from his writings and his investigations as a poet; he had no graduate degrees. The chairman, who shall be nameless, was furious when he discovered this academic heresy, but it was too late. When the time came to name Coutinho, our chairman asked Wagley if the man had a doctorate and Chuck assured him that he indeed did. What he failed to say was that he was an MD and not a PhD. Like so many other Latin Americans Afrânio had followed a course in medicine but never went into practice. Anyone worth his salt in Latin American studies should have known this and that Coutinho and Mejía were more valuable than a whole troop of PhDs.

After I finished translating Afrânio's book I took a quiet bible oath never to do another scholarly book if I could help it, leaving that to those closer to scholarship who would be excited to take on such a task. I am glad to have done this book, however, out of friendship for Afrânio and because big old Brazil sits there ignored as it takes up half of South America and, besides Carnival and Jorge Amado, has a very worthy intellectual side to offer us. Later on I would break my oath to translate Darcy Ribeiro's *The Brazilian People* because even though he was a sociologist, Darcy was also a writer of novels and his book reads like one, even with all of its statistical tables.

JUAN GOYTISOLO

Marks of Identity (*Señas de identidad*, 1966). New York: Grove
    Press, 1969.

SPAIN, LAND OF CONQUESTS BOTH suffered and imposed,
miscegenations that go back before there was history, has most
often been set apart from its expansion, as though Spanish
America were something out of Don Quixote's lands from the
romances of chivalry. "Do you speak the real Spanish?" Non-
sensical misunderstandings like this make it difficult for one to
show that Spain, like England, simply expanded. That's why we
have the aptly named New England and New Spain (Mexico).
It is also why the literatures of the old land and the new blend.
It's a matter of language. The two great baroque poets of the
Spanish language are Luis de Góngora and Sor Juana Inés de la
Cruz, he in Spain, she in Mexico, and their styles are well-nigh
interchangeable. That nineteenth-century outburst of poetry
called *modernismo* belongs to both sides of the Atlantic in an
inseparable way. Try to bring about an estrangement between
Rubén Darío and Antonio Machado and you face failure.
People are doing a lot of talking about magic realism and the
Boom, those signposts of Spanish American writing, but they
rarely bring in Spain. These movements, if such they are, are
but further steps along the path taken by Spanish, or, if you

prefer, Hispanic literature. Where writing is concerned the terms mean the same.

When I was asked to do Juan Goytisolo's *Marks of Identity* I needed just that prod to move me further along out of the reigning sense of separation (I can't calculate the degrees) between Latin America and its Iberian mother countries. Here was a novel that blended in remarkably well with all that I had been doing and reading from overseas Iberia. Goytisolo's antecedents came from both sides of the Atlantic. There is that weird geography which confronted the Spaniards. It was so mythical and otherworldly that they thought it must have come out of those romances of chivalry that drove Alonso Quixano daft, hence the name California. They could think of no better one and it has turned out to be so apt. Magic realism, however, was right there on the Peninsula with Ramón del Valle-Inclán's moody, misty tales described as *esperpento*, a word whose translation awaits another Poe. García Márquez, Alejo Carpentier, Asturias, and Aguilera-Malta all wrote their grim tales of dictatorship that are models of *esperpento*, but the one who wrote the perfect novel of Latin American dictatorship before them was old Don Ramón himself with his *Tirano Banderas* (Banderas the tyrant). It was all one miscegenated culture with local peculiarities here and there.

As I got into Goytisolo's novel I could sense what I have been going on about above. His magic lies in the mood of hopelessness that Spain has suffered so many times, exemplified here in the atmosphere of the Civil War of 1936 and its aftermath. There is an episode of *esperpento* replete with a kind of black humor worthy of Cortázar when a patrol stops a poor gourmet who has been out hunting frogs so he can eat their legs. When asked what is in the moving sack he has in the trunk of his car he replies, "Frogs," and is shot out of hand for sassing the guards. When they get to open the bag they see that, by God, they are frogs, but display not the slightest extenuating remorse. I could only think of García Márquez and the excesses of his Patriarch or maybe Goya's *Caprichos*.

I met Juan only once when I picked him up at JFK and drove him to the Chelsea Hotel. He pretty much let me go my own way with the translation. After I'd made do with the title, *Marks of Identity*, which is not the exact equivalent of the Spanish *Señas de identidad*, closer to an identity card or somesuch, I went along reading the novel and translating as I read, reminding myself that this was Spain and not one of the Spanish American countries I knew or had handled in other novels. This was really very necessary because even though I made myself hear a Peninsula accent as the text went on, the words were pretty much the same as what I had been reading and hearing elsewhere. Can a reader in English who says eye-ther sense that the author says ee-ther? I think not and I wonder if it matters a whit as far as the text is concerned, although it might be important in a case of dialogue, but then only in the reader's mind. The subtle sense of assertiveness in Peninsula speech was caught by Cortázar in what he called "a dialogue between two Spaniards." As I thought about this I found that this same drive is also common among Cubans, perhaps because of their having been closer to the mother country than others were during the formative nineteenth century. I'm always surprised by the fact that my so very Cuban father was actually a Spanish subject until well into his twenties when he became an American citizen. I remember that after the Cuban Revolution Puerto Ricans would complain about the bumptious refugees on their island who were taking over jobs that rightfully belonged to locals. I advised them to buy a pair of marbles and put one in each cheek so they could pass for Cubans, if they could muster up enough hubris.

After the translation came out I was startled and disappointed to find that a substantial part dealing with Álvaro's visit to relatives in Cuba had been left out, with Goytisolo's permission I was told, as he agreed with the editors that the book would be a better novel thereby. It might have been a distraction, perhaps, but I found that the section had relevance to events in Cuba as compared to those in Spain and also that it drew a picture of the close ties between the island and the Peninsula; Fidel Castro's parents were immigrants from Galicia in northwestern Spain, for example. I also remember that Juan had been very adept at capturing the subtle differences and similarities between Spanish and Cuban manners and expressions as he demonstrated how the latter had derived from the former with a measure of acculturation.

I'm not sure whether it was the editors or Goytisolo who initiated the excision. It's still a good novel, but I think it would have been a better one had those pages remained. The whole business reminds me of a parable I once heard regarding an author, an agent, and an editor who were on safari in the Sahara. Having lost touch with the main party, they were struggling through the dunes with a mad thirst and hoping to come across an oasis. When one finally appeared in the distance they stumbled toward it with hopes that it wasn't just a mirage. It wasn't, and lo, there right in its center was a pond of fresh water. While the author and the agent were slaking their terrible thirst in the pond they chanced to look up and there was the editor pissing into it. "What in hell are you doing?" they shouted. "I'm making it better," was his reply.

But the novel is essentially a Spanish story as Goytisolo

dredged up all sorts of historical matter, reaching back to the first Arab invasion and conquest, a theme he would continue developing in the subsequent novels that came to form a trilogy with this one. Again, I didn't have the opportunity to do any of the following ones but they were all well handled. I really don't care to discuss other people's versions because in so many cases they're quite well done and it's only that I would have done something different with them, more evidence that a translator is essentially a reader and we all read differently, except that a translator's reading remains in unchanging print.

MANUEL MUJICA-LÁINEZ

Bomarzo (*Bomarzo*, 1967). New York: Simon & Schuster, 1969.

READING AND TRANSLATING AFRÂNIO Coutinho's study of Brazilian literature was a valuable experience for my chores at Queens College of dispelling ignorance. In like manner when I took on Mujica-Láinez's rich, lush novel *Bomarzo* I not only enjoyed the tale and had fun making sure that my tone was in line with his, but it also served as a chance to revisit and revel in that wonderful world of the Renaissance. No "early modern" for me, how in hell could you revel in anything with such an insipid name?

I was faced with a dangerous situation for a translator as I dealt with a protagonist who was also the narrator of the story. A situation like that is bad enough but there was a further hitch here. Mujica, or Manucho, as he was familiarly known, had set himself into the novel as the mysterious reincarnation of Pier Francesco Orsini, Duke of Bomarzo. This strange and startling revelation helps dispel the reader's wonderment as he comes across references to Proust and other such anachronistic matters from the mouth of a Renaissance Italian duke. The difficulties lap over into the area of the translator's task as he attempts to establish the proper tenor for the tale told by this character who comes from two worlds. The duke is telling his story in twentieth-century Buenos Aires, but the events in which he describes his participation are taking place in an earlier age. Here again I let the words lead me, keeping in mind that I was listening to Manucho retell what he had been doing centuries before when he was the Duke of Bomarzo.

I was aided here by my own search for lost time as I went back to my course on Proust at Dartmouth under the wise guidance of Ramon Guthrie. Mujica relies on a certain Proustian feat of memory although his time had been lost much farther back and his experiences had taken place in a completely different incarnation. He had come up with the whole idea while visiting the Orsini villa, Bomarzo, north of Rome, with its weird figures of monsters in the garden. I had never heard of this strange array before and I regretted having passed it by during my World War II service in the Italian campaign. The origin of the figures is a mystery and Manucho, much as his countryman Borges would have done, decided to write the story of how they came to be, weaving it around the person of Duke Pier Francesco in a tale that mirrors the life of Richard III of England in a great many ways. To do so with the proper magical effect, Mujica makes himself a kind of latter-day paredros of the duke.

Alberto Ginastera wrote an opera based on the novel but it had to have its premier in Washington because the regnant bluenose, machista military dictator in Argentina at the time objected to hints at homosexuality in some places and would not permit it to be put on at the Teatro Colón. Joanna Simon, the mezzo-soprano, had sung a part in the opera and it was she who convinced the family publishing house to take the novel on. I had the pleasure of seeing the opera at Lincoln Center as the guest of the book's editor, Richard Locke, an old Columbia hand. For some reason both novel and opera seem to have disappeared from sight and sound. They merit more attention.

Most of my problems were solved by following Mujica's lead as he wrote a Renaissance autobiography in the twentieth century. He did a perfect job with that perspective and all I had to do was to follow along and see how that arrangement came out in English. I never had an opportunity to do any more of Mujica-Láinez's works because they have been neglected and never offered up for translation. This is a pity because he has one novel that deserves great attention given the pervasive plague of dictatorship in Latin America over the years. Its title is *De milagros y de melancolías* (Of miracles and melancholies) and it is an historical survey of Latin American regimes since the beginnings, all woven into the sequence of rulers of a mythical land called Santa Fe de Apricotina, which gives off sardonic echoes of Argentina and Santa Fe de Bogotá. This parodic string of rulers is a roster of leaders from the origins right down to Fidel Castro. There is no labyrinth for the general here because he is just as big a boob as all the others. The book is trenchantly subversive because, in the manner of all good satires, it strips the emperor bare in all of his incarnations. I remember Ramon Guthrie's telling us, "Proust is fun." Mujica-Láinez shared the Kennedy Medal with Julio Cortázar. I translated both these authors, and it was a lot of fun.

GABRIEL GARCÍA MÁRQUEZ

One Hundred Years of Solitude (*Cien años de soledad*, 1967). New York: Harper & Row, 1970.
Leaf Storm and Other Stories (*La hojarasca*, 1969). New York: Harper & Row, 1972.
The Autumn of the Patriarch (*El otoño del patriarca*, 1975). New York: Harper & Row, 1976.
Innocent Eréndira and Other Stories (*La increíble y triste historia de la cándida Eréndira y de su abuela desalmada. Siete cuentos*, 1972). New York: Harper & Row, 1978.
In Evil Hour (*La mala hora*, 1968). New York: Harper & Row, 1979.
Chronicle of a Death Foretold (*Crónica de una muerte anunciada*, 1981). New York: Knopf, 1983.

ONE HUNDRED YEARS OF SOLITUDE and *Hopscotch* are the two books I have translated that have gone through the most editions and reprints. Even as I write this *One Hundred Years* has suddenly appeared on the lists of best-selling paperbacks in both *The New York Times* and the *Los Angeles Times*, a spot it never obtained when it first came out. This is quite heartening to me as a lover of good literature but saddening to me as a translator. This is because in earlier days translation was "work for hire," like spreading manure on a suburban lawn, paid with

a one-time fee. There was never any question of royalties unless the author involved was Homer or Virgil and the like. It is
painful, therefore, to see an old translation surging along while
I sit here and calculate what I might have been hauling in
had I done it last year. Cass Canfield, Jr., did get me some royalties on the first paperback edition but that went out of print
long ago. There is something on occasion from the Book-of-
the-Month Club, but in general, as far as I'm concerned,
the book might just as well be in the public domain. Let me
stop whining, though. It's too prevalent among translators as,
like so many famished locusts, they pounce hungrily on the
hors d'oeuvres at literary affairs. We must take what small
comfort we can in knowing that we are doing something
honorable in a world of imposters, pretenders, and bourgeois
tradesmen, as old Prince François so aptly put it in *The Fallen
Sparrow*.

As I mentioned before, it was Julio Cortázar who told
García Márquez to wait for me when he was seeking a new
translator for his novel and I was tied up with something else.
It all seems to have worked out to the satisfaction of everyone,
critics included, although there have been the usual occasional
brickbats from Professor Horrendo. This was one of the times,
as in the case of Clarice Lispector, that I had read the novel
before, with no idea of translating it. As in that case I knew I
had something good before me. People who had read the
novel in Spanish were talking about it intelligently, sometimes
not so intelligently, but always with a kind of awe. I suppose
that this should have scared me off, but in matters of translation and a few other things I don't frighten easily and I was
ready to take it on. As I said, this was a book I had read before
translation and I realized that had I followed my usual pattern
the outcome might have been somewhat different. I wonder

now whether that version would have been better or worse and if I were to translate the novel now after having taught it so many times and having read what others said, whether I would be improving on it or only making it worse. All of this, of course, comes down to the fact that every time we read a book it becomes a different one. That's why we can heft, consider, and tolerate version after version of Dante without complete satisfaction but enjoying the reading all the while because the Tuscan is lurking behind the English words.

The immediate problem for me was what to do with the title. A translator must hope that the book he is to do has either one easily translated word for a title or perhaps the name of the protagonist. In some cases the original title is simply out of the question in a different language and care must be taken to see that the solution falls within the spirit of the original. If I may be permitted a mixed metaphor of jargon and military slang, when the target language is missed the critic has naught to do but wave Maggie's drawers. A simple declarative title like *Cien años de soledad* should offer no trouble whatever. Think again. We can pass *de* and *años*, they stand up fine, even though *años* would have to go if we opted for *century*, because that's what a hundred years comprise. I turned that option down rather quickly. *Cien* is our first problem because in Spanish it bears no article so that the word can waver between *one* hundred and *a* hundred. There is no hint in the title as to which it should be in English. We are faced with the same interpretive dilemma as the translator of the *Aeneid* as he starts off with *Arma virumque cano. A* man or *the* man? By Latin standards it could be (and is) both. Virgil didn't have to decide but his translator must. In my case I viewed the extent of time involved as something quite specific, as in a prophecy, something definite, a countdown, not just any old hundred years. What is troublesome, of course, is that both interpretations are con-joined subconsciously for the reader of the Spanish, just as in the Latin example they are for the Romans. But an English speaker reading the Spanish will have to decide subconsciously which meaning is there. They cannot be melded in his mind. I was convinced and I still am that Gabo meant it in the sense of *one* as this meaning is closer to the feel of the novel. Also, there was no cavil on his part over the title in English.

When we come to *soledad* we have a similar bit of ambi-guity, whether it is one of Empson's types or not is still to be ascertained. The word in Spanish has the meaning of its En-glish cognate but it also carries that of *loneliness*, bearing both the positive and the negative feelings associated with being alone. I went for *solitude* because it's a touch more inclusive and can also carry the germ of *loneliness* if pushed along those lines, as Billie Holiday so eloquently demonstrated. Gabo must have liked the choice, too, else he would not have made that outlandish but ever so welcome remark that he liked the En-glish version better than his own original Spanish. There is one claim or interpretation of his, however, that always sets me to thinking. Somewhere he stated that he thought my technique was to read the book through and then just sit down and rewrite it in English. This would be great to accomplish and, indeed, it has been done any number of times when a tale or legend has been turned about and appropriated to create a second masterpiece. My young granddaughter Jennifer has done just this in devising a marvelously Pyrrhonian version of the Hansel and Gretel story where the witch comes off clean. How could it have been that Gabo was thinking of a tech-nique completely the opposite of the one I followed, word by word? In this case I had read the novel first, so there may be an inkling of truth in what he said. Never having written a novel (yet), I am not sure how it is done, but I imagine that plot, theme, characters, the whole conglomeration is there in the novelist's mind and all that is needed is paper, pen, and time. As a matter of fact, this is how García Márquez says he himself did the novel, that it all came together in his mind and he just sat down and strung together the words needed to express it. Maybe in some way I was simply translating in a way close to the way he wrote it.

Opening lines are often the most quoted and remembered parts of a story: Proust's *Longtemps, je me suis couché de bonne heure*; Cervantes's *En un lugar de la Mancha, de cuyo nombre no quiero acordarme*; Kafka's *Als Gregor Samsa eines Morgens aus unruhigen Träumen erwachte*; Dickens's *It was the best of times, it was the worst of times*. So it has been with this book: *Muchos años después, frente al pelotón de fusilamiento, el coronel Aureliano Buendía había de recordar aquella tarde remota en que su padre le llevó a conocer el hielo.* People go on repeating this all the time (in English) and I can only hope that I have got them saying what it means. I wrote: "Many years later, as he faced the firing squad, Colonel Aureliano Buendía was to remember that distant afternoon when his father took him to discover ice." There are variant possibilities. In the British army it would have been a "firing party," which I rather like, but I was writing for American readers. *Había de* could have been *would* (How much wood can a woodchuck chuck?), but I think *was to* has a better feeling to it. I chose *remember* over *recall* because I feel that it conveys a deeper memory. *Remote* might have aroused thoughts of such inappropriate things as remote control and robots. Also, I liked *distant* when used with time. I think Dr. Einstein would have approved. The real problem for choice was with *conocer* and I have come to know that my selection has set a great many Professors Horrendo all aflutter. It got to the point that my wife Clem had to defend my choice (hers too) against one such worthy in a seminar in which she was participating. The word seen straight means to know a person or thing for the first time, to meet someone, to be familiar with something. What is happening here is a first-time meeting, or learning. It can also mean to know something more deeply than *saber*, to know from experience. García Márquez has used the Spanish word here with all its connotations. But *to know ice* just won't do in English. It implies, "How do you do, ice?" It could be "to experience ice." The first is foolish, the second is silly. When you get to know something for the first time, you've discovered it. Only after that can you come to know it in the full sense. I could have said "to make the acquaintance of ice," but that, too, sounds nutty, with its implication of tipping one's hat or giving a handshake. I stand by what I put down in this important opening sentence.

Then there is the measure of sound. In Spanish, García Márquez's words so often have the ring of prose poetry. They are always the right words because their meaning is enhanced by their sound and the way in which they are strung together in rhythmic cohesion. Thus it should be possible to interpret these words/notes from another tongue in the same way that a melody can be passed from instrument to instrument as its essence is preserved, albeit in a different tone. I am rather satisfied with what I have done in this respect and I can look upon my work more as transposing than translating. I haven't looked at other versions of *One Hundred Years* to see how my peers in other languages have done in this respect although I did peruse the one in Portuguese from Brazil. As the mingling of sounds in Brazilian Portuguese has all the tones of a string quartet or more, it is inevitable that the translation from stately Spanish should sing in quite a different way. I use this last description of the Spanish language to point out how Gabo is the direct heir of Cervantes in his instinctive sense of how to use the language. Like the master's, his language will never get stale and I can only hope that my English will carry on in the same way.

For the readers' sake I had to take great care with the names in this book. In order to avoid confusion between father and son (although confusion is subtly encouraged throughout the book) I had to make sure that the old patriarch was always José Arcadio Buendía, never any truncated version, much the way that Charlie Brown is never called anything but Charlie Brown in *Peanuts.* There is some kind of personal essence that must be preserved as we handle names and as the novel progresses this essence becomes clear and the names go on unchanged and exude this essence while taking on new accretions. One's sense of name resists any changes. When I was growing up the President was Franklin Delano Roosevelt, as he always put it, or Franklin D. Roosevelt, not to mention FDR. It rubs against a nerve today when I hear him called simply Franklin Roosevelt. Part of his essence has been left out, making him akin to Franklin Pierce, God save us! What if we went about speaking of John Whittier, Henry Longfellow, Oliver Holmes? Gabo had wise reasons for keeping the name José Arcadio Buendía intact, singling him out in distinction from his son, who was simply José Arcadio, with no surname ever mentioned, and from his great-grandson José Arcadio Segundo. In this last case I chose to keep the Spanish word for second, it being understood as a cognate, thinking that José Arcadio II or José Arcadio the Second sounded too royal or too highfalutin.

The editors added a family tree which they had me concoct for the translation and at the time I thought it a good idea, something to help readers keep all the characters straight and to let them see the complex interrelationships. Later on, after the book had come out, I had second thoughts. If García Márquez had wanted such a table he would have put one in the first Spanish edition. I came to think that perhaps confusion (and fusion) was meant to be a part of the novel, showing how all members of our species look to apes or horses, who would have trouble distinguishing among yahoos. This idea also ties in with the repetition of Christian names in the family, so that distinction is of little import after six or seven generations and a hundred years, when memory dissolves and all who went before become what Turgenev called "gray people." It's puzzling, or is it, since it was put together by academics, that the fine footnoted Spanish edition in the Cátedra series also carries a genealogical table at the beginning.

With the rightfully marvelous reception of *One Hundred Years* by public and critics, the publishers wasted no time in going after more Gabo. I was called upon to translate his first, short novel and a handful of stories. This book had been called *La hojarasca* in Spanish, meaning dead, fallen leaves, but also rubbish, trash, something worthless. I was hard put for an English word that combined all those virtues and pondered long. I finally decided to chance an invention and I called it *Leaf Storm*, thinking about the storm that finished off Macondo in *One Hundred Years of Solitude* and how a similar cataclysm was at work here, turning the town into rubbish. This was the first appearance of Macondo. I wasn't entirely satisfied that I had done the right thing until Alexander Coleman gave me his own unique imprimatur by pronouncing the invention "superb." That was good enough for me.

I wondered at times that I might be messing up in some way because I was translating Gabo's first novel after having done his masterpiece. The order had been reversed and I was concerned that the perfection of *One Hundred Years* might filter into *Leaf Storm* and make it greater than it was. It could be a question of the silk-purse business again, although *Leaf Storm* is far from being a sow's ear or anything like it. Once more I think I was saved by just following the words as García Márquez had put them down and I think the outcome was as successful as translations can ever get.

The stories were varied, but what the cliché would call vintage García Márquez. The fact that some appeared in such magazines as *Esquire* and *Playboy* was good evidence that Gabo was not unknown in North America anymore. His next long novel, *The Autumn of the Patriarch*, was excerpted in *The New Yorker* and therein lies a beautiful tale of editorial timidity and orthodoxy. This novel of dictatorship, a thoroughgoing and intimate look at the workings of the foul, perverted minds of those who practice it, was written without paragraphs and with only an absolutely necessary minimum of punctuation. This is how García Márquez meant to maintain the drive of events, the inexorable momentum of action that makes time move as if viewed from a seat in a passing train as it goes through swamp and slum. I tried to keep the same pace in the translation. It only looked like a difficult chore because the long sentences were run-on, breathless, not the baroque or byzantine ones I would struggle with when I came to translate José Lezama Lima's *Paradiso*. This was too much for *The New Yorker*, however, and they wanted to throw in some paragraphs and punctuation. Since the novel would soon be out in book form untampered with and where the readers could have access to the real thing, and the appearance of a chunk in the magazine would lead readers to the book, Cass Canfield and I went along with the editors, but provided no semi-colons would be forthcoming, with Gabo in mind.

That was only part of the story, however. A word that Gabo enjoys throwing about in a lot of his writing as an expletive but more often than not as a descriptive term is *mierda*, excrement. I have used the euphemism to keep the impact for later. In the translation I naturally used the rightful one-syllable English word when the Spanish term put in an appearance under varying circumstances. It was a favorite word of the novel's unnamed patriarch and as such it was absolutely essential that it appear in English in its correct earthy and expressive translation. This is how I did it, causing great distress at *The New Yorker*. I was given to understand that any number of high-level editorial meetings were held to decide what to do about the word, which had never appeared in the magazine before. As intelligent people the editors saw that the word just had to be matched by its equivalent in English if the truth of the story was to be maintained. Since then I have liked to trumpet the news that in a triumph even greater than his winning the Nobel Prize, García Márquez broke the shit barrier at *The New Yorker*.

The next books of his that I did were stories and two novels, one old and one new. The stories were headed by the novella *La increíble y triste historia de la cándida Eréndira y de su abuela desalmada* (The incredible and sad tale of innocent Eréndira and her heartless grandmother). This was reduced to "Innocent Eréndira and Her Heartless Grandmother," but that, too, was overlong for the book's cover, which said simply *Innocent Eréndira*. There is a fabric woven from the threads of all of García Márquez's work and held together by theme and tenor and, fortunately for the translator, "style." As I look over his collected works I can recognize him in all the ones in Spanish and, although I am an interested party, I think I can say the same for the English. His inimitable kinetic style is everywhere and is skillfully adapted to the varied circumstances of the narration, even in the case of the different worlds of *One Hundred Years of Solitude* and *The Autumn of the Patriarch*. I find satisfaction in the maintenance of this in my translations, although I haven't had occasion to peruse those done by others to see if what I consider his stylistic essence to be found there.

The New Yorker's problem surfaced again in the translation of one of Gabo's earlier novels, if only indirectly. The novel came out in Spanish as *La mala hora* (The bad time), but when he was writing it García Márquez had wanted to call it *Este pueblo de mierda* (This shitty town). No respectable publisher, of course, would have brought it out under such a name. There are those who say that the town resembles Macondo, but I doubt that Gabo fostered any such feelings for his magical creation. It may be that he was showing us the dark side of paradise in more strident terms. As the title ended up, even without the "word," it brought on problems in translation. "The bad time" was out; flat as a pancake. Then I thought of *evil* in place of *bad* and found myself getting warmer. Why not parallel the Spanish and keep *hour*? Finally Milton came to my rescue as I remembered *Paradise Lost* and Satan's entry into Eden. *In Evil Hour* it became and I think it might even have added a necessary dark touch or two of hell and sin.

The last novel I did for García Márquez before he went elsewhere as I was engaged with something else was *Chronicle of a Death Foretold*. In Spanish it had been *Crónica de una muerte anunciada* and my title immediately fell prey to the pedantic pecking of cocksure commentators. It was pointed out that it should been "Chronicle of an Announced Death." I hadn't heard a clinker like that in a long time. I could only think of the late Penn Station and a booming voice announcing the departure of some poor soul to the nether world. The utter absurdity made me even more satisfied with my title and I have been tickled to see that it might even end up as a cliché, as quite often I come across the cutesy phrase "chronicle of a _____ foretold" used in one way or another. I can't see how "announced" could possibly have ever caught on like that.

It was strange, magical perhaps, that after I ceased working on García Márquez I went on to do quite a few things by Jorge Amado and suddenly I got the feeling that Macondo was located somewhere in the State of Bahia, down in the southern cacao country or perhaps more likely on the Recôncavo as the bay shore is called. It was a nice transference and I even began to see Sonia Braga walking down the streets of Macondo while I tried to find her place in the Buendía family tree.

DALTON TREVISAN

The Vampire of Curitiba and Other Stories (Novelas Nada Exemplares. Cemitério de Elefantes, O Vampiro de Curitiba, A Guerra Conjugal. 2nd eds., 1970). New York: Knopf, 1972.

WHEN I WAS IN BRAZIL IN 1962 gathering books and knowledge, along with the already mentioned Clarice Lispector and João Guimarães Rosa I also heard talk about and picked up a book by a newcomer named Dalton Trevisan. I was drawn to the book by its title, *Novelas Nada Exemplares*, a play on Cervantes's *Exemplary Novels*, though on the negative bias here. It may have been that Trevisan wanted to point out that Cervantes, too, could have been playing around with the title in an ironic way. Trevisan's stories are succinct slices of existence and their horror is the horror of reality as opposed to the fictional realism that his predecessor and more subtle mentor Machado de Assis disdained. In his collection *The Conjugal War* the stories, brief though they be, are meant to reduce heroics and sentiment down to the essential nastiness of close relationships, something he calls the domestic *Iliad*, the worst of all. I keep thinking that in some ways his repetitive couple, João and Maria, could well be the true un-Homeric picture of Zeus and Hera, not to mention the Adam and Eve we never hear about.

On my return I chose one of the stories, "The Corpse in the Parlor," for inclusion in *Odyssey*. It wasn't just my own ghoulish taste that drew me to it, but it also found a spot in editor Saul Galin's sense of black humor. I translated the story and found that I had to make sure not to render the language too expansive. The story might verge on the repulsive for some, but it's told in normal, direct terms, which is Trevisan's style. A daughter is lying on her bed pondering her dead father laid out in the adjoining parlor. He had burned her with her cigarette once when he'd caught her smoking. Now, puffing away, she gets up, goes to the parlor, pushes the rosary beads aside, and applies the burning tip of her cigarette to the dead man's hand. There's no magic here, only stark realism, but I wonder if magic realism can't be divided like magic itself into black and white, so that what we have in these stories could be a fine psychological example of black magic realism.

The title chosen by the editors, *The Vampire of Curitiba*, is likewise not at all exemplary. There is no Bela Lugosi or Borgo Pass here. The *vampire* is a sad, neurotic twenty-year-old pining over the impossibility of love. For the uninitiated, however, the word vampire is mysterious, even exotic, and it could be that the foolish protagonist is kin to the creatures. People also must be thinking that Curitiba is the next town over from Macondo, in some never-never land, and not the large industrial city it is, capital of the state of Paraná, directly south of São Paulo, about as exotic as Cleveland. Dalton Trevisan is showing us how what we consider to be the most banal aspects of existence are so truly awful that they, too, can seem magical, albeit of the darker variety.

I never found any problems with the translation of these stories. There was very little stylistic variation and once I was in tune with them I was able to handle the jabbing style properly. In the João and Maria encounters I had to be careful with the dialogue and the insults tossed back and forth, trying to keep the tone as it was in the original and neither softening nor sharpening it too much. I never met Dalton, but I was told that he was rather reclusive as literary figures go in Brazil, tending to the family ceramics business and rarely leaving Curitiba for São Paulo or Rio. We did correspond, however, and he looked over all the translations. I found something here that I hadn't encountered with any other author. Dalton was never satisfied with what he'd written. If we compare the first edition of one of his collections with subsequent ones we will find all sorts of changes in the text. This carried over into the translations as he made substantial changes that had nothing to do with my translation. Luckily, no Professor Horrendo caught this, maybe because Dalton's stuff wasn't to his prissy taste or perhaps, and this I hope is so, Brazilian literature doesn't attract his kind.

Like Machado de Assis, to whom I have compared him, Dalton Trevisan has suffered from a lack of outside attention. Machado has begun to receive his just due as his translations prosper somewhat, but it has taken too long. I hope that Dalton will be picked up and appreciated more in years ahead, even if he is picked apart and deconstructed, although I don't know how you can deconstruct a skeleton. I'm not all that optimistic, however, when I think of Machado's natural succesor, Lima Barreto, who is still largely unknown outside of Brazil. I did my bit in his case, however, translating his Machadian story "The Man Who Knew Javanese" for *The Oxford Book of Latin American Short Stories*.

JOSÉ LEZAMA LIMA

Paradiso (*Paradiso*, 1968). New York: Farrar, Straus & Giroux, 1974.

As I was doing *PARADISO* I thought at times I was translating Proust, although it had to be a tropical, baroque Combray. Lezama was difficult to translate because of his wealth of words and the translator had to be careful with each one. The richness of his vocabulary was matched by the wealth held by each individual word itself. Lezama Lima was also one of Cuba's leading poets when he decided to write his novel, and he had the poet's feel for the juice in every word, hoping that the reader would be able to squeeze out every drop, even though the seeds might be left behind to mystify. He was an intense critic and explicator as well, so I had to think quite hard at times to figure out whether or not there was something hidden in a word and if there was, what it might be.

Julio Cortázar, a good friend and protector of Lezama's, was one who had brought the novel to international attention, and it was he and Carlos Monsiváis who edited the Mexican edition. I followed this because the first one done in Cuba was full of flaws. Since then notes and other things have turned up posthumously and changes have been spotted, but I can't see any great urgency for a new translation because of this. The best thing might be to do a variorum edition (an academic I once knew thought that the plural was *variora* and even said so in print). This same process might also serve Dalton Trevisan's stories and it would provide meat for those interested in how tales are put together.

Lezama, *el gran gordo*, as Julio lovingly called him, had held some official literary positions after the Revolution, but *Paradiso* didn't endear him to the macho homophobic (there must be a better word) leadership and he was pushed aside. He could have left Cuba but it was too much a part of him so he stayed on. Political matters did interfere with the progress of the translation, however. Mail service between Cuba and the States was well-nigh impossible, but here Julio Cortázar came to the rescue as the good friend and promoter of Lezama's work. I would send pages of my translation and queries to Julio in Paris; he would pass them to a friend at the Cuban embassy there; then they would be sent on to Lezama via diplomatic pouch. The process would then be reversed and I would be able to incorporate corrections and suggestions into the translation. The system was working quite well until Julio protested some literary malfeasance on the part of Fidel and became *persona non grata*.

I didn't have much trouble with José Cemí, the protagonist, but I had to be careful with the voices of his friends Foción and Fronesis, omnipresent in some sections, for they had to be subtly distinguished in their definition, much like Settembrini and Naphta in *The Magic Mountain*. I was able to imagine Cuban voices by thinking of my father's expressions and talk and those of Cuban relatives I had visited long ago. These Proustian reminiscences were of great help in this ever so Proustian novel. Help was also there in the person of the Cuban poet Mercedes Cortázar (no relation), who helped in the editing of the manuscript.

A posthumously discovered novel, *Oppiano Licario*, has surfaced. This is the character whose death at the end of *Paradiso* gives continuance to José Cemí. The book most certainly should be translated and even though I haven't read it I'm not sure that I'm up to the task at this point. Let a younger Proustian, if there be such around after deconstruction, undertake the job. I can only hope that if the book is done the title will be retained. I was pleased that the Italian *Paradiso* was kept for my translation, but then, Roger Straus was at the time one of the few Magi left in commercial publishing. *Paradise* would have been a loss and since the Italian word was used in the Spanish and not *Paraíso*, why translate the word in an English version and ruin the effect. Beyond the obvious Dantean connection, it was said to be the description that the purported Italian Christopher Columbus had given the island of Cuba.

Demetrio Aguilera-Malta

Seven Serpents and Seven Moons (Siete lunas y siete serpientes, 1970). Austin: University of Texas Press, 1979.

On my second trip to Brazil in 1965 I went via Mexico and Peru to see people and to visit Machu Picchu, anxious to see if Pablo Neruda had really misspelled the name. In Mexico the exiled Puerto Rican writer José Luis González, whose work we had published in *Odyssey*, asked me if I wanted to attend a talk by the Ecuadorean writer Demetrio Aguilera-Malta. His name had come up several times in a course at Columbia with Andrés Iduarte and I knew his novel *Don Goyo*, where there were inklings of what was to be called magic realism. Naturally, I went. After his talk, the subject of which I've forgotten, I got to talk to him and he invited me to lunch at Sanborns the next day. It seems that he wanted to talk about Brazil. He'd been cultural attaché from Ecuador in Rio some years previous, and it was there that he'd met his wife, the Mexican writer Velia Márquez, who had been serving at her embassy. We talked about his friend the Brazilian poet Jorge de Lima and all kinds of Brazilian matters. This was the beginning of a beautiful friendship.

When the time came for my wife Clementine to write

her doctoral dissertation in Spanish American literature at Columbia, I thought of Demetrio. He needed more attention as the younger generation was getting all the play. Also, he would be of great help as she would be in touch with the author himself. The result was a continuation of visits with Demetrio and Velia in New York and Mexico and finally the publication of Clem's book *Demetrio Aguilera-Malta and Social Justice: The Tertiary Phase of Epic Tradition in Latin America* (Fairleigh Dickinson University Press). In her study she shows how the thing that came to be called magic realism had its start with earlier writers like Aguilera-Malta and Asturias as they used their novels as voices calling for more freedom and justice and were the traditional voice of a folk, as the epic had been in past times and those poems had evolved into the novel. In this way there was a continuum of collective expression. Magic realism in particular gives us the heroes and archetypes of epic in a different guise, but the age-old struggle is maintained. In the course of her work on him, Clem also brought out some translations of hers from some of Demetrio's shorter works.

In 1970 Demetrio published what I consider to be his best work and his defining novel, *Siete lunas y siete serpientes*. It grabbed me so tightly that I had to translate it, even if I hadn't been asked to do so by any publisher. This could have been quite an unwise decision, as I came to find out with subsequent projects. The novel reveals Demetrio's deep wisdom and his epic and mythical perception of Latin American reality. There are all sorts of subtle revelations of how life is lived in those countries with a bit smoother but still Swiftian deftness. If there is one book that defines what has been called magic realism this is it. García Márquez made the term famous and vice-versa, but I say that the great master of the genre, if such it is, is Demetrio Aguilera-Malta.

At the start, of course, there was the natural business of the title. *Siete lunas y siete serpientes* scans nicely in Spanish, but "Seven Moons and Seven Serpents" is a dud in English. "Seven Moons and Seven Snakes" is even worse and also lacks the fine semantical nuances of the prior term for the slithery creature. My solution was simple enough, a bit of reversal so the title would scan in English too: *Seven Serpents and Seven Moons.* I'd learned a good deal about handling the surreal and the magical from doing Asturias's *Mulata,* although Demetrio's magic does have a greater touch of the real about it and appears to be more cogent and therefore magic *realism.*

The characters are quite a bit more outlandish than those of García Márquez and I didn't find their fellows again until I came upon them in the Azores in the novel by João de Melo, *My World Is Not of This Kingdom.* The trick with outsized characters like these is to make sure that the dialogues and descriptions are as real as they are in the original and at the same time letting it be seen that something magical is going on, deceptively real though it may appear. Of course, here again to the point of boredom I can only say that I follow, quite aware that the translator is the squire of the arts, but comfortable with the fact that it was Sancho Panza who made Don Quixote possible. All the others were bent in one way or another on deconstructing him back into Alonso Quixano and in the end they lost him for us.

Demetrio was a man of many parts and as such was a delight to be with. Clem and I had many an insightful hour with him and Velia. His first book was actually a collection of drawings done in Panama during one of his many exiles and it is noteworthy that after a lifetime of literary activities he took up painting again in later years. We have a remarkable painting of his in our study that shows a young Indian girl astride a jaguar, something straight out of *Seven Serpents* and as colorful literally as his descriptions are figuratively. Demetrio had settled down in Mexico because, as he put it, it was much easier living in Mexico and returning to Ecuador in good times than living in the opposite situation. When his nephew Roldós Aguilera became president of Ecuador he named Demetrio ambassador to Mexico, which brought him well-deserved perquisites and saved him from the literary grub work that often took him away from his real writing.

Demetrio's early political activities, which had sent him into exile so many times, made for an ironic twist in the story of the publication of *Seven Serpents* in English. While I was working on the translation I got a request for an interview from *The Wall Street Journal*. It made the front page and was noticed down in Texas. I had spoken about Demetrio and how at the moment I was translating his latest and best novel as a labor of love, without a publisher in mind. I got a subsequent query from the University of Texas Press which led to its publication and its later appearance in a popular edition in the fine Avon series of Latin American writing. One of the founders of the Socialist Party in Ecuador had gained his first recognition and publication in the United States under the indirect assistance of that firmly capitalist organ *The Wall Street Journal*.

Three of the authors I have translated went on to become good friends of Clem and me and we had a great deal of personal contact with them. These are Julio Cortázar, Demetrio Aguilera-Malta, and Luis Rafael Sánchez. It isn't that I wasn't friendly with the others, but there weren't those relaxed moments of cabbages and kings and various elixirs, listening to my old jazz 78s with Julio, talking Brazil with Demetrio, and enjoying Luquillo beach with Wico (Luis Rafael Sánchez). I've tried to figure out if this type of relationship is of any help for

a translator beyond direct questions, whether a sense of near-
ness lets me hear the voice of these particular people as I interpret their words. If I am the translator I am supposed to be, it
really shouldn't make any difference and yet I do hear their
voices along with their personal pronunciations and intona-
tions. This is that misty world of translation that is hard to describe. We can feel it or sense it, perhaps, and get an idea of
how things take place there, but description is difficult. Even
Sor Juana had trouble figuring it out. This may be why people
like to call such things magic realism.

Demetrio went on to write another novel that put him in
that circle of Latin American writers who dealt with dictator-
ships. It is *El secuestro del general* (The kidnapping of the general), which came out in English as as *Babelandia*, the name of
the mythical republic where it takes place. I didn't do it because, as usual, I was deep into something else. It's hard to say
which dictator is more repulsive, Aguilera's skeletal figure here
or García Márquez's fleshed-out monster in *The Autumn of the
Patriarch*. Their souls are kindred, however, and they are shared
by Alejo Carpentier's Cartesian tyrant in *El recurso del método*,
oddly translated into English as *Reasons of State*. These novels
form a kind of category or sub-genre that in distinctive ways
gives a glimpse of what might be a facet of the Latin American
psyche or "soul" through the brutes who have ruled the place
so often. Aguilera-Malta may have done it best by showing the
bleak black magic behind the fearsome reality.

Avalovara (*Avalovara*, 1973). New York: Knopf, 1979.

I WISH THAT I COULD have met Osman Lins before his too early death in 1978. I did meet his wife, the writer Julieta de Godoy Ladeira at a PEN conference in Rio and it was comforting to ponder him from what she had to say and from his warm and elegant letters, which gave me a better understanding of his complex book. *Avalovara* is the title in Portuguese and as in the case of *Bomarzo* it behooved us to carry it over into English. It is said to refer to one of the incarnations of the Buddha, the compassionate one, if I heard right. I found that the complexity of the book neither hindered nor helped the progress of my translation and as in the past and especially and wisely with difficult books I let Osman lead the way. My Cortazarian experiences did serve me well in keeping on the track, as the novel was put together much in the manner of *Hopscotch*, although here the reader doesn't hop back and forth, even if he might well think he does. The novel's structure is based on a spiral and a square as the spiral passes through the letters of the square, which make up a two-dimensional Latin palindrome: SATOR AREPO TENET OPERA ROTAS. It says that the plowman holds his wheels firmly in the furrow and according to what the book says it can also have reference to God's governance of the universe. The palindrome goes back and forth and up and down.

It was my early impression that the book was more difficult to read and understand than to translate. What saved me was the realization that Lins, as writers must, knew exactly what words were needed as he put them down. In this way it was not really too difficult to follow him and put down what he was saying into English, although at times I had the feeling that I knew what he was saying and could render it but couldn't always grasp the full sense of it. Here is a book that deserves a second reading. The second time around I caught on to what was up and I was pleased to see that my translation had captured things without my having been fully aware that first time of what he was on about. The second reading enlarges the book as it lays open the scope of it. This is really the complete opposite of so much writing that people want to call post-modern (I must consult my dog on this as he's an expert when it comes to posts), which instead of being enlarged on a second reading withers away to wind.

One feature of the novel that gave me pause as a reader but not so much as a translator was the fact that one of the three women with whom Abel becomes involved has no name but is represented by the symbol ʘ. This was easy to translate, I simply reproduced it. But when I came to read it I was stumped. I would do a kind of gag and finally ended up just calling her "O." That was inadequate and is evidence that we do need to imagine vocal cords and move our lips as we read to ourselves. I wonder how Saint Ambrose would have handled it. Here Lins goes beyond any notion of the impossibility of translation and gets into the impossibility of expression itself if we push it too far.

If Julio Cortázar had his paredros, Lins has come up with

something even more complex, something he calls a *iólipo*. It is a being encased inside another from birth, an ingrown twin, imbedded, as it were. What is the translator to do with it? Since Portuguese has done away with the letter *y* and the word does have a Greek sound to it, looking something like polyp, I went ahead and called it a *yolyp* in English. Again, the reader may have trouble understanding what it's all about, but I think that anglicizing the word brings it at least a little closer to home, closer to an understanding, or a conjecture at least.

After *Avalovara* another of Lins's novels was brought out called *The Queen of the Prisons of Greece*, which I didn't do. I did do a story about a remarkable elephant named Hahn, as mysterious and seemingly as symbolic as the characters in *Avalovara*, which appears in *The Oxford Book of Latin American Short Stories*. As has been the case with so many of the books I have translated, I am disappointed and saddened that *Avalovara* has not received the attention it is due. Perhaps it is because of its purported difficulty; maybe I expect too much of readers and have tarried too long in the company of those of us who find Proust fun. *Avalovara* is certainly more fun than trying to break Enigma or some run-of-the-mill double transposition cipher. I wonder what Tom, "the fun-loving Rover," would have thought of it, or of *Hopscotch*, or, yes, of Proust.

LUIS RAFAEL SÁNCHEZ

Macho Camacho's Beat (*La guaracha del Macho Camacho*, 1976).
New York: Pantheon, 1980.

A DELIGHTFUL AND SATISFYING source through which I have
become acquainted with both the works and the person of
authors I have translated is the one offered by my former students. It was María Cristina Rodríguez who brought to my attention so many good writers in her Puerto Rico. Even before
Clem and I began what would be a yearly Hajj to that fine
and forgotten isle, María Cristina got me to reading Luis
Rafael Sánchez and Rosario Ferré. Then when we finally got
to San Juan she introduced us to them both. I translated
Rosario's fey little story "The Littlest Doll" and then I em-
barked on what was to be both a challenge and a romp, Luis
Rafael Sánchez's *La guaracha del Macho Camacho*. Although I
had read it and celebrated it, as I began to work on it I had to
ask myself what the hell I was going to do with it, this unique
piece of writing that all by itself explained and justified Puerto
Rico. Clem and I spent time with Wico (this is how his little
nephew tried to say Tío Luis and it stuck) on wonderful
Luquillo beach at the eastern end of the island, and we all got
to work on it.

I have said many times that I simply follow the words of

the author, but I neglected to say that in so many cases I have to follow the rhythm of those words as well. This novel's words are strung together more or less in the rhythm of its titular *guaracha*, a dance and a song, doubly rhythmical in both sound and sensuous motion. Here, once more, we come to the title. What can you do with *guaracha?* It would have to stand as it is, no more translatable than samba, fox trot, or tarantella. It could be that the only ones who knew what the word meant were those who had been denizens of the Palladium in the fifties. As we pondered this, Clem, who'd been there, hit upon the solution: what about *beat?* Everybody knows what beat is, even rock has a beat, monotonous though it may be. Jack Kerouac had tried to use the word in a rather different way, but those of us back from the wars were known to feel beat. The Krauts were beaten, we were just beat. And there were the Beatles, far-removed from any *guaracha*. All of this might then be included in the word, for better or for worse. Lamentably it would do away with the alliteration between *guaracha* and Macho. The novel covers a lot of ground, however, and this fact was a part of Clem's idea. In the book we follow Macho Camacho's song about as it leads the various characters along their way as they follow a route, a beat, as it were, like a cop's.

Language not only breaks down into the very personal way one uses it, but also into certain structures reserved for the clan. In *Macho Camacho's Beat* I had to be careful of these slots and try to keep the translated words in their proper place. In the case of Benny, the wastrel son of Senator Vicente Reinosa, storming through the streets in his beloved Ferrari pursued by the *guaracha*, I was able to get close to American slang because his circle was already into a kind of vulgar acculturation, the gabble of those the Mexicans used to call *pochos* when they came back from Los Angeles. We must remember, however, that Dante found such speech eloquent, and showed it as he wrote his *Commedia* in what was the common rendering of Cicero's stately tongue. It was with the street talk of the masses that I had to be on the watch, thinking back to days in San Juan and imagining what that talk would have sounded like had those same people been speaking English as their native tongue. It's that fine distinction between a gaucho sounding like Gabby Hayes and a truly English-speaking one as we translate the *Martín Fierro.* This is an impossibility that can only be approached, never overcome. I was pleased to know that Piri Thomas thought that I had succeeded as he classified the translation as *chévere.* I shall not attempt to translate that wonderful Caribbean term supposedly derived from the French *chevalier.*

There is something in the book, however, that is almost as troubling and ineffable as the pronunciation of ʘ in *Avalovara.* What does the *guaracha* that pervades the book as its very essence sound like? I remember giving thought to that same problem to a lesser degree in *Hopscotch* when faced with Berthe Trépat's playing of the "Pavan for General Leclerc," by Alix Alix. I have found that I lack the originality needed to imagine new melodies. Maybe it's because my head is too crammed with the melodies of others, both the good and the bad, for there to be room for anything new, but I'm not too sure how originality works in any case. This leads me to the thought that just as every reader reads a different book, so, too, he or she will imagine a different melody for the *guaracha.* What a songbook could be compiled if we could harvest them all.

The song is pervasive throughout the book and gives it its rhythm. Indeed, as I translated I had to keep this in mind and make the prose flow much in the way Góngora made his poetry flow so that the meaning could be found in the rhythm itself. This is an extremely active tale as we switch from scene to scene and act to act. Benny's Ferrari has a motion that translates the *guaracha*, and the words it seems to embody, "Life is a phenomenal thing," are put into action. Popular song and poetry seem to be couched in the same rhythmic pattern as popular speech and Wico's use of the vernacular or, better, the near-vernacular as he regularizes it into a kind of national idiom, blends in nicely with the song being blasted over the radio. The problem of rhyme came up with the repetitious slogans concerning Benny's father, the senator. They go *"Vicente es decente"* followed by a rhyme in *-ente*. I made it *"Vince is a prince"* followed by a rhyme in *-ince*. I'm still not entirely satisfied with it but it was the best I could do after many attempts.

This is the only thing I've done by Wico although Clem has translated a short piece of his called "Getting Even." More of his work needs to come over into English. The influence of the *Guaracha* can be seen in the fact that soon after a boxer named Camacho surfaced and was immediately yclept Macho. I made no attempt to translate the term in the title because it, too, had become part of a name, and the word itself has become part of the English lexicon in the battle of the sexes. In Spanish animal husbandry, where the term is most legitimately used, it simply means the male of the species. Its usage for male humans is meant to show strength and resolve, but then it drifts into negative tones in *machismo* which, like all -isms, acquires an additional sense that renders it risible for right minds. All of this hovers behind the name and can be interpreted in ever so many ways.

JUAN BENET

A Meditation (*Una meditación*, 1969). New York: Persea Books, 1982.
Return to Región (*Volverás a Región*, 1967). New York: Columbia University Press, 1985.

MY PENCHANT FOR NOVELS OR writers considered "difficult" by some may simply be another matter of circumstance. Not reading a book before digging in, as is my wont, would seem to preclude any sense of its being difficult. It so happens, however, that a majority of the works I have translated seem to offer trouble to a lot of readers. Maybe my experience in cryptography is what leads me willingly into these thickets, or perhaps it's just been fated for me to be there, although I have little belief in fate or any such thing this side of a black hole. What I can say about these books is that it was most often fun doing them.

I only heard of Juan Benet when I agreed to do *Una meditación*. What drew me to him right off was his Catalan surname (like mine, and akin to Stephen Vincent's) and the fact that somewhere I'd read of his being called "the Proust of Spain." Later on someone properly corrected this by calling him "the Benet of Spain." The lack of paragraphs in the book didn't faze me one whit as I first saw it because I had been through *The Autumn of the Patriarch* and *Paradiso*. There was no trouble here because there was a flow that simply resisted paragraphs. I could see why Benet had been called the Spanish Proust, not so much for his search for lost time as for his ability to keep that flow of words moving along smoothly through a time that was both then and now and a place that was both here and there. As I compare the texts of the two Benet novels I did I'm pleased to find that they form a whole, a single piece of work, really, the way Proust's two *côtés* conjoin.

The books I did were translated in reverse order. *Return to Región* had been written first, followed by *A Meditation* as an aftermath. I suppose one might say that the order in which I did them made it easy for me, for when I got to the earlier work where he began I was on to all his tricks. Actually, I found that it made little difference. The books are quite similar as to time and place, differing only in what changes in the blink of an eye, a crucial moment (the Germans say it so well with their *Augenblick*) or in the nanoseconds between the light's striking an object and our catching its image. If I wanted to make a cheap comparison I could say that Región was Benet's Macondo. It sounds nice, but Región is his very own and needs no Macondo or Erewhon to explain it. Besides, I can't imagine seeing Sonia Braga sashaying down its streets as I could see her doing in García Márquez's town. Benet has squeezed the essence of Spain's regions and their regionalism into one area, and what better name for a place than something straight out like Región? Only for a split second did I consider Englishing it by dropping the accent. The effect would have been ruinous.

Strangely, by doing the second book first I was able to understand more easily many things when I got to the first novel. In any case, I was pleased to find that my rendering of the two books came out in a homogeneous way in spite of the time that had passed between the two translations. One could flow very easily into the other. This could mean that Benet's style was constant and it could also mean that during those intervening years nothing radical had happened to change my perception of his words and ways. I may have become different in some tiny ways but his words were strong enough to endure and let me catch them in their firmness. I do wonder, however, whether I could say that after a thirty-year gap. If I were profligate with what little time I have it might be fun to go after *One Hundred Years* or *Hopscotch* again and see how they would come out, but I have better things to do, like rereading Proust and wondering if I could get to write like a piece of yellow wall.

I met Juan a couple of times, once in New York for a reading of *A Meditation* and again in Lisbon at a Wheatland Foundation conference. I recall an episode from that time when at lunch the Spanish novelist Torrente Ballester was going on about how smoking and bullfighting were two good macho traits that explained the Spanish character. Juan, who was never tauroscatic, put in that he was a chain smoker and that he detested bullfights. I could see a new Spain in the works and I wish that Juan could have kicked his habit of the filthy weed and not have died so early. I always wondered if he really did remind me of Bela Lugosi in his looks or whether it was due to the spell of mystery that pervades both novels. As far as I know, these are the only works of his that have appeared in English. On the strength of these novels I think that anything hanging around should be done and done well.

VINÍCIUS DE MORAES

The Girl From Ipanêma (*A Garôta de Ipanêma*). Merrick, NY: Cross-Cultural Communications, 1982.

MARCUS VINÍCIUS DE MELO MORAES was born in 1913 at a time when his mother was reading or had just read Henry K. Sienkiewicz's *Quo Vadis*. I came across his poetry on that first trip to Brazil and later heard him sing and recite on some records I had bought. In addition to being a fine poet he was also a good singer and was involved in the development of *bossa nova* with Antônio Carlos Jobim, Baden Powell, and others. In his official life he was a foreign service officer and really was an agent for good relations when he would show up at various *boîtes* around the world. Vinícius (I never met him, but everybody always referred to him by his first name as is customary in Brazil when public people have the love and respect of everyone) was also the author of a play, *Orfeu da Conceição*, which was made into the movie *Black Orpheus*, with substantial changes.

   Stanley Barkan of Cross-Cultural Communications has been publishing an excellent series of chapbooks over the years, including some of my own poems and Clem's translations of the work of Julio Ortega and Francisco Arriví. One day he asked me about doing someone from Brazil. I consulted with my old student Roy Cravzow, who is continually back and forth to Brazil, and we immediately thought of Vinícius. His song "The Girl from Ipanema," done with Tom Jobim was already a hit here (Tom, the nickname for Antônio, is pronounced something like *tone* and not *tom*). So we took that as a title that would catch people's attention and we put together a small anthology. Some of the poems are long, some are short, all are touched with both serious and merry overtones.

I particularly like "Creation Day," an irreverent romp that takes off from Genesis and comes to an end worthy of Machado de Assis. The theme is Vinícius's feeling that God should have rested on the sixth day instead of the seventh, thereby freeing mankind from its onerous existence. I wonder if he could have picked up the germ of that thought from Machado's *Posthumous Memoirs of Brás Cubas*, where Nature/Pandora tells Brás that she is both his mother and his enemy, the latter for having given him existence. With both writers this gloomy thought is put across in a way lightened by Brazilian *jeito*, which sees the essential irony in the matter and finds it rightfully amusing. I wonder what Dostoevsky would have sounded like had he walked the streets of Rio rather than those of St. Petersburg.

"Elegy Almost an Ode" is a similar poem where Vinícius mingles the intents of both forms. This, too, has echoes of the wild careening ride of Brás Cubas astride a hippopotamus when he comes to meet Nature during his delirium at the start of Machado's novel. It also might explain why Vinícius worked so hard at having a good time and how Brazil is not the Eldorado envisioned by Voltaire but, rather, the one Epicurus might have come up with had he set his mind to it.

This is the only book of poetry I have translated, although

I have done quite a few individual pieces for one collection or another. As I look back it seems that they were mostly Brazilian and with time, despite their differing moments and places, I can sense a kind of similarity that goes beyond mere language, as if language can ever be something mere. I can't spot any great difference in my intent here from that in translating prose as, once more, it becomes a matter of words. There is an occasional quest for rhyme, which can be handled if done judiciously, but I don't think Frost was thinking only of rhyme when he slapped translation down. He was wise enough to see its inherent impossibilities. I do find that with a language in which I am rather weak, like Russian, I do know just enough to enable me to read poetry along over so many unknown words and yet get to understand it in some ways better than in an English translation that is loud and clear. If people go for the left-hand pages of this wisely bilingual Cross-Cultural Chapbook 34 I think they will catch what I am going on about.

LUISA VALENZUELA

The Lizard's Tail (*Cola de lagartija*, 1983). New York: Farrar, Straus & Giroux, 1983.

MANY YEARS AGO AT Columbia during my graduate student and instructor days, I was editorial secretary of the *Revista Hispánica Moderna*, edited by Don Federico de Onís. I would also write some of the brief reviews we published and at the same time keep an eye out for possible material for *Odyssey*. Since my dissertation had to do with black characters in Brazilian fiction and sometimes elsewhere, by preference I would pick out fiction to read and review as the books came in, looking for possible clues. I can still remember over the years an Argentinean novel called *La casa de los Felipes* (The house of the Felipes), by Luisa Mercedes Levinson. It was a family chronicle set in Buenos Aires with all the byways and intricacies of the genre. At the time I had been reading the impressive novel *Crônica da casa assassinada* (Chronicle of the assassinated house) by the Brazilian Lúcio Cardoso and the similarity intrigued me. Quite some time later, at a PEN conference, I believe, I met the author, a wonderfully charming grande dame of the Argentine mold. I was delighted to meet her after having thought quite highly of her novel. Then she gave me the great surprise of telling me that she was Luisa Valenzuela's mother. Knowing her in both capacities was doubly rewarding.

I had done *The Lizard's Tail* by then and Clem had done some short pieces by Luisa. Her novel is completely different from her mother's but both books share the consummate skill of the fine writer, and the two women share a graciousness, each in her own way, that bespeaks an intelligent knowledge of people and how they feel, something akin to what in Spanish is called *don de gente*. I am pleased that the women writers I have done have been so consistently good. I wish there had been more of them. Maybe, like General Lee, I prefer the company of women. I had come to know Luisa and had been with her at various gatherings before I took the novel on, so I was quite pleased when asked to do it. This was one of those few times when I translated a novel from the original manuscript, as it hadn't come out in Spanish yet. The title I worked under was *El Brujo Hormiga Roja Señor del Tacurú* (The Red Ant Wizard, Lord of the Tacurú). This was mercifully shortened to the symbolic title it came to bear. I am intrigued with the succession of *wizard* and *lizard*. The last time I saw that confusion was with W. C. Fields in *Million Dollar Legs*.

This book must also be included in my short list of "difficult" works, not so much for the difficulty in translation, although there were moments, as for difficulty in reading. Since I translate as I read, the difficulty in reading was assuaged by the translation process. As the translator goes along pondering words he or she must perforce put more time into the reading and quite often what appears to be a difficult text becomes almost self-explanatory, just as my rusty Latin thus slows me down with Roman writers so that I think I am probably getting more out of them than when I skimmed along with Miss Whitford. In the case of this novel I was fortunate in being fairly well-versed in the doings of Afro-Brazilian *candomblé* and its *orishás*, which helped guide me properly through certain magical passages.

There were others, however, where Luisa's own imagination was doing fine work and I had to watch my step. Experience with Osman Lins and Juan Benet was of great use here. Knowing what had been going on in Argentina during those frightful decades was also of great help in keeping my mind alert as to where the action was coming from and where it was going. Translating fiction is sometimes analogous to interpreting intelligence reports, and with a Research and Analysis Section at hand the matter can be either tedious or treacherous as far as facts and fancies are concerned. As a teacher of Latin American literature and kindred matters over the years I have accumulated enough knowledge to carry me through with my own R & A Section, just as FDR was often the only one in the War Room who knew where a certain island was because he collected stamps. I, too, have collected stamps and I even have some from Southern Asiatic Georgia. These are stickers my mother used to get from the Saint Anthony's Guild, inscribed S. A. G. and which my picaresque older brother Deet (Jerome) would pass off and trade as coming from the above-mentioned mythical country, as fine a piece of fiction as I've seen in many a year. How is it, though, that his victims were so obtuse as not to realize that Southern Asiatic Georgians most likely didn't speak English? Here and there I have come across similar cases of deliberate fraud perpetrated by translators, but I've always let them off the hook because it must have been fun for them thinking they were getting away with it.

Jorge Amado

Sea of Death (*Mar Morto*, 1936). New York: Avon, 1984.
Captains of the Sands (*Capitães da Areia*, 1937). New York: Avon, 1988.
Showdown (*Tocaia Grande*, 1984). New York: Bantam, 1988.
The War of the Saints (*O Sumiço da Santa*, 1988). New York: Bantam, 1993.

When I began work on my graduate studies in Brazilian literature I was far from imagining that one day I would be translating some books by one of the principal figures in my dissertation, Jorge Amado. Several of his books had already been done and even after I began doing translation others were taking care of him. Finally, when his agent Tom Colchie called and asked me if I wanted to do some things for the Avon Latin American series I was delighted. I liked his books and I liked the Bahia he wrote about, actually the Bahias, the city of Salvador da Bahia and the southern part of the state of Bahia where he had been born and where the cacao barons were prospering and laying the ground for many of his novels with their feuds and violence. Although he came from that southern region and his father had migrated down there from the state of Alagoas, Jorge made his mark writing about Bahia

the city, as natives of Salvador tend to call their town. He became deeply involved in the Afro-Brazilian cult of *candomblé*
and its whole pantheon of Yoruban *orixás*. The third stop on
my first trip to Brazil after Belém and Recife was Bahia and I
nosed around the places I had read about in Amado's novels. I
had hoped to meet him but he was elsewhere at the time. My
explorations of his turf, his mise-en-scène did serve my imagination well, however, and I remembered those days as I
worked on translations of his books.

My geographical and topographical knowledge of the
scenes of my translations is varied. When I did Cortázar I had
no firsthand experience with Paris, Buenos Aires, or Vienna. I
could envision the Lima of Vargas Llosa's second novel, having
been there a couple of times, but Piura and the jungle of *The
Green House* were as mysterious for me as García Márquez's
Macondo. It was all magic realism. As I said before, I was never
in Bomarzo but I had lingered in Italy for a couple of years
helping to retrieve it from the Germans and I also had a pretty
fair acquaintance with and a liking for the Renaissance, so I
was on rather safe ground with Mujica's novel. My memories
of Havana and Cuba were quite remote by the time I got to
Paradiso, but I do remember having some recall of Cienfuegos,
my father's hometown, when I got to the Cuban portion of
Goytisolo's novel, the chunk that was eventually left out of the
translation. Although I've never been to Curitiba, the Brazilian
cities are the ones I know best, having spent more time there
including two years in Rio, living in Copacabana on the Rua
Barata Ribeiro. I'm not sure whether or not a lack of personal
acquaintance with the scene of a novel matters that much if
the descriptions are good. If not, I can't see that it makes any
more difference than it would have had there been a detailed

description of the sights on the streets of Macondo, to the ruination of the varied impressions brought forth by all those different readers.

The first book I did by Jorge Amado was called *Mar Morto* (Dead Sea) in Portuguese. This just wouldn't do in English because of the obvious biblical connotations as well as possible Palestinian ones rife at present. Strangely, this is not so obvious in Portuguese. The book is quite sentimental, "touching," and poetic, describing the life of those who sail the *saveiros*, the sloops that ply the broad and sometimes dangerous waters of the bay from which Bahia derives its name. Since Guma, the protagonist, dies a heroic, useless, and somewhat inevitable death at the end, *Sea of Death* was not too bad a choice of a title for bringing out the spirit of the tale. *Candomblé* is involved, for to die at sea is sweet (*é doce morrer no mar*) as one enters the living arms of Iemanjá, the Mother of Waters (Yemayá in Afro-Cuban *santería*), one of the more tender *orixás*. The African background is quite evident and sometimes dominant in all of Amado's books about the city of Bahia. It appears in *Captains of the Sands*, a story about a gang of urchins in Bahia, with a tone of both warmth and despair quite similar to that of *Sea of Death*. In these books I had to be careful with slang words and also be on the alert when it came to terms from *candomblé*. In this I may have had some spiritual help as Jorge had written me that on a certain New Year's Eve he had lighted a candle on the beach in honor of Iemanjá for me. Regionalisms abound in Brazil but unfortunately they are dying out because of the influence of television and radio as they purvey what could be called "general Brazilian," much like its counterpart "general American" in the United States as it works the same kind of erosion on local manners and speech.

These two novels were from Amado's earlier phase when

he was also writing stories about the cacao country and the "colonels" there in their battles for land and people. He returns to the region for his later novel *Showdown*, the next to the last. The title in Portuguese was *Tocaia Grande* (Big ambush), the name of a settlement which grew into a grand city, much like José Arcadio Buendía's vision of the future Macondo. That original name would have meant nothing to the American reader so the editors opted for something a little more understandable and one which does convey a good deal of the spirit of the novel. One of the main characters, if not the protagonist, is Fadul Abdala, a Lebanese immigrant. This immigration was quite widespread in Latin America during the nineteenth and twentieth centuries, producing a new type of character for a new reality. Since these Lebanese arrived during the time of the Ottoman Empire, they bore Turkish passports and thus were called *turcos* throughout Latin America, much in the same way that Spanish immigrants were called *gallegos* because so many of them came from Galicia in northwestern Spain. What is the translator to do with these terms? Readers in Spanish and Portuguese know who they really are, although some might think that these Lebanese really are Turks even though very few of this last ethnicity ever reached their shores. (Near Eastern Jews were also subject to the term because of their passports.) In most cases where the text said *turco* I went along with Turk, letting the context explain who they really were, feeling that it fit the tone of the original, as in *One Hundred Years* and its Street of the Turks. In *Showdown* Jorge Amado has variations and Fadul is sometimes called Arab, even Maronite.

The language of the backlands is perforce as violent and as colorful as are its inhabitants. In this book I had to watch out both for the meaning and for the spirit of a great many words.

It has been said that people who deal with animals, drovers and the like, have the richest vocabularies of curses. I could see that in this book. Once more I had to follow a tight and sometimes impossible course. There had to be something of the colorful original in what I wrote but also, and perhaps even more important, I had to maintain the spirit, angry, jocular, and so on. I'm not entirely happy with the variants I came up with. Maybe if I'd been in the old cavalry instead of the infantry I would have had more success. I was also stumped at times for synonyms for the male member. I found that after I had exhausted what I thought was a rather formidable array of Anglo-Saxon terms, Jorge kept right on going with new versions in Portuguese. I was hard put to find anything that could match the eloquence of *estrovenga*.

In his last novel Amado returns to the city. The title settled on by the editors was one of Jorge's own alternatives, but it can be a little misleading even though it may be understood once the novel has been read through. In Portuguese the prime title was *O Sumiço da Santa* (The disappearance of the saint), admittedly awkward in English no matter how it might be twisted or turned. The story does involve two saints although they are one and the same person, Saint Barbara in Christian tradition and the Yoruban Yansã (Yansan here to make it easier for the typesetter and the English-speaking reader). The story is a beautiful mingling of the two religions and Jorge shows that they are really one and the same, although we might sense a preference for the African aspect. After all, Jorge was an *ogum* or acolyte in the *candomblé* of Mãe Senhora, the most authentic and most respected priestess in Bahia. Since the Afro-Brazilian element is so dominant, I found that more often than not I had to leave a lot of terms as they appear in the original. Any attempt at translation would have robbed them of a great deal of essence. To support this a glossary was appended, which could even have been of great help to Brazilian readers down in São Paulo or Rio Grande do Sul, not to mention readers over there in Lisbon. The story takes place during the military dictatorship Brazil suffered in the sixties and seventies. Brazilians called their militarists "gorillas," thus adding another grain of confusion to the origins of the Spanish word *guerrilla*. I was living in Brazil during part of that dismal time so that the official claptrap appearing in the novel was quite familiar and I knew what it was trying to say or cover up and I did my best to reproduce it in English, relying also on my knowledge of Washington-speak during much of the same period. There is also a French television crew in the book who are arranging for the filming of a "typical" Brazilian carnival in Bahia, out of season. I've always wondered if Amado might not have been poking some fun at the French-directed movie *Black Orpheus*.

I kept missing Jorge Amado in Brazil but finally did meet him in New York at a book party for his last novel. By then the young revolutionary who had written his first novel at the age of seventeen was the grand old man of Brazilian culture, so sacred that the gorillas never dared touch or even criticize him. His novels have become a fine combination of the lighthearted and the essential, never solemn, never sanctimonious, fun to read, though I can almost say not as much fun to translate, even when it is a labor of love. I still await Sonia Braga's version of Saint Barbara/Yansan. Only she can do it.

OSWALDO FRANÇA, JÚNIOR

The Man in the Monkey Suit (*O Homem de Macacão*, 1972). New
York: Ballantine, 1986.

THE MONKEY SUIT IN THIS novel is a set of mechanic's coveralls, which strangely carries the same name in Brazilian popular parlance, *macacão*, from a like simian root, *macaco*. There
could be a problem since monkey suit in English can sometimes apply to other forms of *indumentaria*, as my father liked
to say. I think I have heard it used for a tuxedo or full dress, although these now seem to go under the names of black tie
and white tie in contemporary speech. I do miss the good old
"tux" from junior-prom days. Uniforms are also apt to receive
this appellation, or could it be apelation? Coveralls are really a
fuller version of overalls. I suppose the *c* in it *c*overs everything
while overalls don't quite make it. In New Hampshire these
last were more often than not called "overhauls," which was
what you wore when working with a "wheelbarrel" full of
cow "badure."

I'm sorry that this novel didn't get much attention in
translation. It's the story of ordinary people and their travails in
lesser Brazilian cities. It could be that for foreign books to be
successful here there has to be some scent of the exotic or
strange. That, too, can be lost in translation along with Mr.

Frost's poetry. Maybe that's what happened here, given the fact that the story is narrated by the protagonist, the aforementioned mechanic, who is struggling upward toward ownership of his own garage. (A word of warning must be made here to those used to translating from the Spanish. In Portuguese the word for shop or garage is *oficina*. It doesn't mean office; that's *escritório*.) The language, then, has no glint or glow to it and it's what we might expect from such a person. Because of this I had to be careful not to fall into any poctization or to gild what he was saying. Maybe the flat quality of the first-person narration held no attraction for English-speaking readers. The story itself is as good as any an American writer might tell. What if the mechanic had been the narrator in *The Great Gatsby*.

There is one egregious error that appears on the very cover of the American edition. The mechanic is referred to as Alfonso. This name has always been a problem for people who come to Portuguese from Spanish. The *l* has disappeared in Portuguese, most likely because of the dark, glottal way the Portuguese and Brazilians pronounce it, the same as the Russians. The name is Afonso, sans *l*, and there were so many kings of both Spain and Portugal who shared the name that the Alfonso/Afonso variation is a good way to tell them apart. This misdeed could only have been a hypercorrection on the part of the editors. This is the sort of intellectual hubris that translators can easily fall into if they are not wary and accordingly humble. They should never be so proud as not to consult the dictionary when there is the tiniest inkling of doubt. I fell into this haughty position myself some years back when I took the liberty of "correcting" the name of the Cuban painter Wifredo Lam into Wilfredo. Luckily, Julio Cortázar caught it, with no word of admonition, as was his wont, and I was spared humiliation. Since then I have seen Lam's first name misspelled many times and I catch myself uttering a pedantic tut-tut or the mental equivalent thereof. I am no doubt compensating in that way for my own erroneous hubris.

ANTÓNIO LOBO ANTUNES

Fado Alexandrino (*Fado Alexandrino*, 1983). New York: Grove/ Weidenfeld, 1990.

The Return of the Caravels (*As Naus*, 1988). New York: Grove Press, 2002.

"What Shall I Do When Everything's on Fire?" (*Que Farei Quando Tudo Arde?*, 2001). Awaiting translation.

THERE ARE THOSE WHO SAY that since the Nobel Prize was ticketed for Portugal a couple of years ago it should have gone to Antunes instead of José Saramago. This is standard fare every year after the prize has been announced, but I might just go along with it, not because I don't have high regard for Saramago's great work but because I find Antunes's strange, baroque, and sometimes surreal world more to my taste even though I like the other man's magically real one too.

Here at the outset I have to make some niggling remarks regarding nomenclature in order to dispel the ignorance that abounds regarding Portuguese names. With Portuguese surnames, the opposite of the Spanish, the first is the mother's and the second the father's. This is the norm in spite of a widespread custom in Brazil of doing whatever you want with your name. The author here must therefore be called Antunes and not Lobo, although Lobo Antunes passes muster. Some may also note that António bears an acute accent here (-io is not a diphthong in Portuguese) while in Brazil it is written Antônio with a circumflex. This is because the *o* is open in Portugal and closed in Brazil. This matter brought me much puzzlement and indecision when I was working on Padre Vieira, Sor Juana's bugbear, born in Portugal, reared in Bahia, and claimed by both countries, rightfully. My singularly silly solution as a neutral outsider was to call him António Vieira if I was dealing with his activities in Portugal and Antônio Vieira when he was working in Brazil. Let it be António Lobo Antunes, then, and let pedantry be laid to rest.

I first became aware of António when one of my fine former students, Elizabeth Lowe, translated his novel *South of Nowhere*. Here we are faced with editorial timidity because the title in Portuguese is *Os Cus de Judas* (The assholes of Judas). Staid Portugal, still imbued with forty years of the clerico-fascist Salazar regime, was able to shake it all off and display that blatant title on the cover of the novel in bookstore windows. The novel is the story of the hard go the Portuguese troops had of it in Africa during the colonialist wars, in which Lobo Antunes served as a medical officer. Since it's a military environment, it's a shame that the editors here weren't prepared to go all out and give the book a title based on an expression I remember well from my own days in uniform (in Texas): The Asshole of the Earth. It would have fit in perfectly with the tone of the book.

Some time later Tom Colchie, Antunes's agent, asked me if I would be interested in doing something by him. I looked over the ones in question and settled on *Fado Alexandrino*, the fattest one, a thorough look at the situation in post-revolutionary Portugal with flashbacks into times gone by. It covered the activities of a group of veterans of the colonial wars who had come together for a kind of reunion after the revolt against Marcelo Caetano's Salazarian government. As with all collective narrations, the translator has to make sure that each voice has its own tenor, and that they don't all end up sounding like the voice of that monotonous vocal robot called Voder or something like that at the 1939 World's Fair. To do this I had to listen carefully to how António put down what his characters were saying. I also had to get to know them individually in order to ascertain and also to imagine what that particular person would have to say had he been speaking English. Also, as the transitions move quietly from one speaker to another, I had to stay on the *qui vive* and not put the right words into the wrong mouth.

Lobo Antunes belongs to that large array of writers I have done who can be called "difficult." As with the others, my advice to readers is simply to read, approach him once again as though he were Góngora or as though they were listening to one of Beethoven's late quartets through sheer hearing. These problems or difficulties (I'm not sure which they are, and there is a difference) show up in an even more severe form in the second novel of his that I did, *The Return of the Caravels*. Here he has boldly blended the homecoming of veterans and colonists from Africa with the return leg of Vasco da Gama's voyage to India. Cervantes and Camões both appear out of the past in a modern setting. I tried to match some of the odd archaic spellings with something that might purport to work in English: Lixboa/Lixbon, reyno/realme, for example. I'm still not so sure that it worked out that well.

I got to know António during a couple of trips to Portugal and once at the Wheatland Foundation conference in Lisbon that I mentioned a while back where he was a somewhat reluctant participant. His charming wife, Maria João, allowed to Clem and me that António could be difficult at times. She was breeding a race of dogs that were said to be descended from Roman mastiffs and local wolves and we had occasion to go to a dog show in Sintra with them. Clem and I were amused but Maria João was not as António treated the affair as he would an athletic match or maybe a burlesque show, making audible remarks about the various canines and their caretakers. He obviously saw them as disparate and amusing characters, canine and otherwise, for a novel. Since Lobo Antunes is a psychiatrist by training I have wondered perhaps if he hasn't dipped into his files on occasion to extract some notable figure for his novels. I have just promised Tom Colchie that I will soon get started on António's latest book, a great, fat monster of a work which is the novelized life of a famous Lisbon transvestite, Joaquim Centúrio de Almeida, who went by the name of Ruth Bryden. The title is *Que Farei Quando Tudo Arde?* (What shall I do when everything's on fire?). I shan't fool with the title until I get the translation under way.

With the translation of *Fado Alexandrino* I was aided enormously by Maria João, who went over it checking every dot and tittle since António had had done with it and told me to do it in any way I saw fit. These feelings are quite akin to my own. When I finish a job to my satisfaction (I really mean dissatisfaction) I'm ready to let the editors do with it as they will, even if that includes urination. As can be seen, nothing was done with the title. The *fado* is the great popular song of Portugal. The word is said to come from the same root as *fate* and the songs, most especially when sung by the great Amália Rodrigues, inevitably invoke that longing or nostalgia or whatever that the Portuguese and Brazilians call *saudade*, which could also stand in as an explanation of the *soledad* in *One Hundred Years*. I am still puzzled by the *alexandrino*. I can't see where the iambic pentameter fits in, nor can I see any connection with Lawrence Durrell's work. My best thought is that António is taking the *fado*, the raw material of his tale, and making it classical in the mode of French alexandrines. I'm content to let the readers have a go at their own interpretations. As for *The Caravels*, the editors more than likely picked up on the French title, as that translation had come out first: *Le Retour des caravelles.* The title in Portuguese is *As Naus*, deceptively simple. It might mean nothing but *The Ships*, but *nau* implies a larger craft, a man-of-war or a merchantman. Here we have to give thought to that stinging wretch called a Portuguese man-of-war who can ruin a good summer swim, but I would rather let it rest right there. The ships of Columbus and Vasco da Gama were caravels, so I find the title well-chosen.

Lisbon has its own slang and popular usages and one who translates from both Portugal and Brazil must of needs be wary, given the longstanding and somewhat mutual isolation of the two entities. Only in recent times when Portuguese refugees from Salazar and later on Brazilians fleeing the gorillas might seek asylum in each other's country have their kindred cultures moved closer together. I've been given to understand, however, that Portuguese parents have become dismayed to see their children picking up Brazilian accents and ways from the many *tele-novelas* coming out of the larger country with its greater facilities. Portuguese teenagers find it "cool" to go about mouthing Brazilian slang and such. Still and all, the lexicons are really still quite a bit apart, even to the very word for slang, *calão* in Portugal and *gíria* in Brazil. I am fortunate in having two different slang dictionaries, one for Portugal and one for Brazil. An example of the dangers in these discrepancies can be found in the word *bicha*. In Lisbon it means a line, a queue, in Brazil a drag queen. The mystical part of my mind wonders if the English translations I have done could be identified, author and locale unseen, as being Portuguese or Brazilian. I would have trouble myself, I do believe, but in this business we pride ourselves on being cosmopolitan and universal, or we should.

JOSÉ DONOSO

Taratuta—Still Life with Pipe (*Taratuta—Naturaleza muerta con cachimba*, 1990). New York: Norton, 1993.

I FIRST CAME TO KNOW about José Donoso when I read his great novel *The Obscene Bird of Night* and could almost see how Luis Buñuel would have gone about filming it as I read. Buñuel had a knack for showing us what we might have missed as readers. I'm thinking about his work with Benito Pérez Galdós's late and most adventurous novels, which served him as the basis for *Nazarín* and *Viridiana*. These films were most revealing of the Galdós we had missed in college when we were put through *Doña Perfecta*. I would even venture that Buñuel could have squeezed out of this last-mentioned novel whatever arcane Galdós lay hidden behind the banal text. It has always been my notion that with *Nazarín* Galdós was giving us his *Quijote*. In the case of Donoso's novel, however, there might not have been any need for Buñuel. It was as though the novelist himself was already giving us the film as he primed the cameras of our imagination. I also knew about Donoso from his literary memoir *The Boom in Spanish American Literature*, a consideration and explication of many of the books and authors I would subsequently be dealing with.

It was at a talk of his at the Americas Society where I finally met Pepe in person. We had a grand chat and shortly after that I ran into him again at the Dartmouth Bookstore in Hanover, New Hampshire. Clem and I were visiting my mother up on the Lyme Road and, as usual, we stopped by the store to browse and get a summary of local happenings from manager Wilbur Goodhue, a schoolmate from Hanover High. There among the books was José Donoso, whom we'd just left in New York. He was at Dartmouth that summer as a Montgomery Fellow and was living in Sara Castro-Klarén's house. Pepe and Pilar invited us to dinner and we spent a fine evening talking about friends and writers we knew, some of whom I had been working on. Donoso's health was fragile and I worried about him but he managed to hang in and keep on writing for quite a few more years. We would come together from time to time and I was delighted finally when Norton asked me to do his two novellas. The last time I saw Pepe was at the book party for the translation in New York.

Taratuta is narrated in the format of an historical investigation, fact and fiction mingling in a tale that begins during a period of Lenin's exile, with a character named Taratuta, whom the narrator is trying to track down in history and tie in with some rather odd people and events in present-day Latin America. There is a decidedly Borgesian ring to the whole matter. What I had to be careful about was the mixture of history and fiction, not to gum up any real information about the life of the Russian exiles. I had to be equally careful, of course, with Donoso's invented facts. The author can blend and bend fact and fiction, the translator cannot. In this story, fictional as the core is, one is never sure if even the fiction is accurate, whether or not there may be some lying within the fiction itself, and, as Érico Veríssimo's grandfather used to tell the Brazilian novelist, writing fiction is nothing but writing lies. What we might have here, then, is a lie within a lie. Two negatives can make a positive in mathematics, so could this be a way to lie oneself into the truth? I'm not sure where translation stands in all this.

The second novella, *Still Life with Pipe*, takes its title from the painting that serves as the crux of the story. Once again we have a situation where, in a sense, truth comes out of a lie or, we might say, a lie develops into the truth through its own insistence, much after the technique of Paul Joseph Goebbels, who kept on saying (!) "If I say something three times it's true." As with *Taratuta*, we never know exactly how this is developing and I had to be careful of the transitions and also with the people involved in them. Once more, since there are paintings in question, the reader (and the translator) must make use of his or her imagination to picture the pictures. When the question is raised as to whether they are masterpieces or junk, we have to go on imagining what they might look like in either case and we can view them in the same way that we listen to Berthe Trépat's pavan or Macho Camacho's *guaracha*.

I remember one decision in the translation that led me into broader considerations: what to do with street names. In this case it was Calle 18, 18th Street. The English translation would immediately remove the thoroughfare from Santiago de Chile and place it in the Chelsea district of New York or some other city in the U.S. where a like system is used. I tend to preserve the original designation, keeping *calle, rua, avenida*, and such. If I had left it at Calle 18 I would have had a mongrel version for a person with little or no Spanish. Calle Eighteen sounds terrible. The simple solution was to write out 18 in Spanish, Calle Dieciocho, making it sound more true. Also, there are some numbered thoroughfares that have taken on a certain personality behind their enumeration: Fifth Avenue, Forty-second Street. The same obtains for any number of streets in Latin America. Bogotá is loaded with *calles* and *carreteras* that bear numbers for names and each is known for its own unique characterization.

This is the only book by Donoso that I have done. I would have liked tackling *The Obscene Bird*, but it was in good hands and the version put together by Hardie St. Martin and Leonard Mades stands up. As to this last case, I'm never sure how collaborative translation works, being pretty much a lone wolf in it all myself, but in this case it worked out fine. I was once asked to fix up a translation and I tried, but in the end I just went about translating it over from scratch. In another case I was asked to "look over" a translation and I just had to turn it down because, again, my urge was to do my own version and that wasn't what they wanted.

IRENE VILAR

A Message from God in the Atomic Age, rereleased in paperback as *The Ladies' Gallery* ("The Sirens, Too, Sang that Way"). New York: Pantheon, 1996.

ONE DAY A LOVELY YOUNG woman came to my office at Queens College. She had written a book, a memoir, and wanted me to translate it into English. I was doubtful, as I always am when approached to take something on, but, also as usual, I was easily charmed into saying yes. Irene is the granddaughter of Lolita Lebrón, one of the Puerto Rican nationalists who shot up the House of Representatives during the Truman years. The book is a memoir of the intertwined and difficult lives of Irene, her mother, and her grandmother. Had it been a novel, and it reads like one, it would have been a remarkable family chronicle and a fine *Bildungsroman*. I set about doing the translation and found that I was going along as though I were doing a novel, which was precisely the right way to proceed. The work was made easier by the fact that I knew the protagonist of this "novel" personally. It was the same as it would have been had Tolstoy really known Anna Karenina (but of course he had).

Puerto Rico has always stood high in my affection and esteem and I called upon my memory of places and people to govern the accuracy of what I was doing. I had already done *Macho Camacho*, so a lot of the environment was already there in my mind. A great difference between the two books is that here, the main character is also the narrator, so that the voices are more limited in range than those in Wico's novel. This would be helpful for the translator as I strove to keep the range of tone even.

I translated from the manuscript and I'm not sure whether the book has come out in Spanish or not. It should. The title I worked with was something Irene had picked out from Kafka's story "The Sirens," "The Sirens, Too, Sang that Way," which ended up as the epigraph for the published book. When it was brought out the memoir was called *A Message from God in the Atomic Age*, which was the title of a poem Lolita had sent to President Eisenhower, bringing about her transfer from prison to St. Elizabeth's Hospital in Washington, giving the impression that poets are mad, since Ezra Pound did time there. When the book was reissued in soft-cover the title had been changed to *The Ladies' Gallery*, from where the group had opened fire on the legislators. Evidently the first title smacked too much of a devotional homily from the likes of Billy Graham or some other bible-whacker.

Irene had attended a school in Orford, New Hampshire, for a time. This lies some twelve miles north of where I grew up; she was fortunate in having me as translator because I was able to straighten out a few geographical details that must have been vague in her memory. Along with this I could imagine the Puerto Rican scenes because I'd been there so many times, and there were no particular problems with the New York area, my habitat for most of my adult life. I had to derive the atmosphere of Spain from what I'd learned from my books and also my experience with Goytisolo and Benet. Irene's own coverage of the peninsular episodes was quite clear and offered no problems.

Irene and I have been in touch every so often and I know that she is working on a novel. It should turn out well, I think, because this memoir has all the qualities that make for good fiction. I recently had an e-mail passed on to me from her as she tried to get in touch. The problem is that I am disconnected, as it were, still enjoying the splendid isolation and peace offered by that blessing. The only web sites I'm logged onto are those maintained by our arachnid friends as they go about their duties of catching flies. I do look forward to her novel and I can sense that it will be something good for her, for Puerto Rico, and for those of us who still like to turn pages.

A God Strolling in the Cool of the Evening (Um Deus Passeando pela Brisa de Tarde, 1994). Baton Rouge: Louisiana State University Press, 1997.

Before the Zeitgeist soured and went into reverse as Exxon began undoing all the good things Teddy Roosevelt had done to oil and gobbled up Mobil, this last company had sponsored a literary award called the Pegasus Prize after its symbol of the Flying Red Horse. The prize was given to literary works from countries where Mobil had interests. The juries were made up of literary types from both the United States and the country in question. The winning book, more often than not a novel, would then be translated under the largesse of Mobil and published by Louisiana State University Press. I served on one of these juries as we considered works from Latin America. The hundreds of entrants were winnowed down to a few finalists from among whom we made our choice. That year we chose *Rasero,* by the Mexican Francisco Rebolledo. That novel dealing with past times intrigued me because I found points of contact with *Bomarzo.* I was working on something else at the time and I was glad to see that it passed into the hands of Helen Lane who Englished it superbly.

Some time later I got a call from Mike Morgan, the man

who laid on the whole Pegasus show, telling me that the country of choice that year was Portugal and asking me if I would be willing to take on the translation of the winner. I was particularly interested in things Portuguese and this strange novel of Roman Lusitania caught my fancy. I knew that I would have to watch my step because the story took place during the second century A.D., when Marcus Aurelius was emperor, and my Gibbon was a little rusty. I had resuscitated my Latin when I took my qualifying exams for the PhD and now I could bring it back once more after years of slippage and disuse. I would be writing contemporary English, just as Carvalho had been writing contemporary Portuguese, but the people who were speaking it had lived ages ago and there must be no hint of anything modern like the jet trails that have ruined shots in any number of historical movies. I was preceded and led in this by the author, who had maintained his text in a prose that was chronologically neutral and yet fit the story perfectly. I also faced the danger of slipping into archaisms because of the flavor of what I was reading. Latin may be archaic for us but it was completely contemporary for those who spoke it.

I did have to break with the Portuguese regarding names, however, for like the other Romance languages Portuguese translates or modifies classical names into contemporary forms. Although English does the same with biblical names, we tend to preserve those in Latin, although we are also most likely to Latinize names from the Greek. In a way, then, I was retrotranslating as I put the Portuguese versions back into what had been their original Latin forms. I also had to follow the changes in sound that had come about with these names and act accordingly. Póncio didn't become Poncius but went all the way back to Pontius, as in Pilate. The main female character is Iúnia in Portuguese and in her case I found myself between Junia, thinking of Junius Brutus Booth, no doubt, and Iunia without the accent. By using Iunia I kept the Latin sound, although Junia would have sounded the same there in Latin, but not in English or in Portuguese.

It is not my business in translation to correct inaccuracies in matters historical, so any errors along those lines must be chalked up against the author. One mistake was pointed out to me by my old classmate from Hanover High and Dartmouth, the eminent classicist and divine John Pairman (Jock) Brown. In one scene Lucius, the narrator, is reading a scroll. Jock allowed that a Roman patrician would never do any such reading, but would have it done for him by a slave. Had I known this when I was doing the translation it would have put me into a quandary. A change of that nature was textual and would mean much more than a word or two different, like my solution with Asturias when I turned Geo into George or making minor adjustments with Irene's faulty geography of Orford and its environs. I have maintained that if Homer nods in the Greek he should be made to do so in English. So far I haven't caught any flak in the matter except for Jock's spotting the mistake, so I guess I've gotten away with it for the nonce. I mean the author has. I'm not so sure about posterity. I can only hope that someone will pick up on it because that will mean the book is being read. I only met Mário once, when he was in New York for the book's launching. I did enjoy doing the book and getting back into Roman times. The title is rather unwieldy in both languages and I wonder if it might chase readers away, but I only change titles when asked.

The Posthumous Memoirs of Brás Cubas (Memórias Póstumas de Brás Cubas, 1881). New York: Oxford University Press, 1997.

Quincas Borba (Quincas Borba, 1891). New York: Oxford University Press, 1998.

With the welter of praise and encomia that has come my way for my work with so many fine contemporary authors, it still wasn't until I did two of Machado de Assis's masterpieces that I felt fulfillment as a translator. My other writers, being pretty much of one or two generations, might be said to be still on literary probation. I've been around long enough myself to see changes in ideas, intents, and tastes that have made me wonder whether or not I should reconsider certain things, but I am thankfully stubborn enough to cling to my own set of notions, which I feel have developed and mutated enough and with which, furthermore, I am comfortable. So I leave my cherished contemporaries at the mercy of change, happy with the chance to have worked on an author who can be termed a classic.

When Oxford University Press inaugurated its Latin American series it was a great eye-opener and revelation for many whose literary experiences had never partaken of a lot of fine books from the south. A very few were known, some translated, but most often as part of the restricted world of specialists. There's more to be found in Latin America than what has come out of the here and now. Machado was one of the greats who had broken through the barrier of ignorance, but even then probably only because of the prod of interest in later writers, starting with Borges. The two novels I translated had, indeed, been done and not so long ago. I found the versions quite acceptable but I could never accept the asinine titles assigned them in an evident attempt to render the books a bit more explicable and approachable at the start for readers far-removed from things Brazilian. *Epitaph of a Small Winner* is a rather small-minded summary of what Machado was up to and it falls short of his intentions for his character of Brás Cubas, whose very name might have had extended symbolic connotations: Brás—Brazil, Cubas (kegs)—drunken expectations. *Quincas Borba* was not named for the main character, Rubião, but for the mad philosopher who links the two novels together in an important way while sharing his name with his dog. *Philosopher or Dog?* is rather simplistic if not downright simple-minded. There is the chance that Quincas might be Rubião's alter ego as Rubião, too, goes mad.

Machado de Assis was a great admirer and one could even say follower of Laurence Sterne. The style of *Brás Cubas* shows this. I had read *Tristram Shandy* years ago and as I looked over my translation I could see remembrances, but this must have come from Machado's text itself because my weary memory could not possibly have brought forth something that I'd read so many years ago. In fact I remember having read it on board ship, either going overseas or coming back after the war, in one of those wonderful little paperbacks that were distributed to the troops and had all the classics in the series. The translation did show me, however, that I must have been reasonably faithful to the original and to Machado's style, into which Sterne must have filtered. I'm pleased that this came about quite naturally as Machado led me along. I also think that my translation somehow conveyed his Pyrrhonean skepticism. Although my own attitude along these lines is close to his, I think that any such feeling here is purely Machado's.

When I came to *Quincas Borba* I had to watch my tacking (one never sails straight with Machado). In his follow-up novel he narrates the story himself. First of all, Rubião was probably incapable of telling his own tale as Brás Cubas had done with his ultramortal wisdom, and, secondly, I don't know how Rubião would have handled things after he lost his wits. I had to keep in mind here that the voice was Machado's and not one with which he had endowed a character, supernatural or otherwise. There is nothing supernatural or ghostly about the late Brás Cubas, of course. One of the delights of the novel is the fact that Machado never explains how a dead man could be telling his tale, leaving it up to us to imagine or just take it as it comes. Maybe this could be called magic realism, but Machado probably wouldn't have liked magic realism any more than he liked realism itself, which he abhorred in the name of reality as he pointed out so sharply and, one must say, so cruelly in his put-down of Eça de Queiroz's *Cousin Basílio*.

In *Brás Cubas* I was faced with two versions of the same man: Brás the protagonist of the story and Brás the supernatural narrator. Although they are ostensibly the same person, circumstances had to make them different. As we read along we get to see that Brás the subject is a rather mediocre person, one might even say dimwitted at times, while the other Brás, of course, has the wisdom of one who has no future and has experienced what has been called the moment of truth.

Luckily for me the mortal Brás didn't have too much to say during the course of the novel so I wasn't too hard-pressed to distinguish between the different manners of speech of the two. The dead Brás has, of course, been endowed with the genius of Machado de Assis as he finds out what a proper Charlie he was during his lifetime. At this point I can only hope that I got the incarnation and the excarnation both rightly placed.

The fact that Machado is really speaking through Brás Cubas's ghost can be seen as narrator Brás and author Machado describe the doings and antics of Quincas Borba in both books. As I recorded the story of the dotty philosopher in them I could see that there was coincidence in the style of the descriptions, which means that they were being offered in the same voice. I imagine that we could carry this along further in search of the essence of narration, but it would be about as rewarding as the mental masturbation offered by crossword puzzles.

There is still much in Brazil that should be brought to the attention of English-speaking readers, even though we now have most of Machado's stuff. There are the works of Afonso Henriques de Lima Barreto, Machado's natural successor, even though Lima Barreto claimed to disdain the earlier writer. We also have the wild poet Sousa Andrade, who linked his surnames and wrote as Sousândrade. His long poem of the odyssey of an Inca prince, Guesa, takes him all over the world, including the United States, which is the scene of his "O Inferno de Wall Street," a bilingual hodgepodge of New York in the 1870s with all the hanky-panky that was going on then.

I came to Machado de Assis late as a translator and I think it was meet. I had read him, studied him, and taught him. I had the translation of a number of novelists behind me and I like to think that, unlike Lear, I had reached the goodbye decades with a modicum of wisdom. Nowadays as I look away into the distance I can see that I have reached the age where everything beyond a hundred yards is all Monet, while once it had been Courbet. There is compensation, however, as the vistas of my imagination became Hieronymus Bosch, one more bit of evidence that old age is the baroque moment of existence.

ANA TERESA TORRES

Doña Inés vs. Oblivion (*Doña Inés contra el olvido*, 1992). Baton Rouge: Louisiana State University Press, 1999.

MY SECOND AND WHAT MUST be my last involvement with the Pegasus Prize once offered by Mobil came when I translated the first novel I had done from Venezuela, so fortunate with oil and so unfortunate with poverty. I have never been to the country but I was kept abreast of local ways and goings on by my brother Jerome, who spent a couple of years in Caracas handling his export-import affairs. Although this is the first Venezuelan novel I have done I have had longstanding thoughts about the possibilities offered by the works of my old professor from Columbia days, Arturo Uslar Pietri, and I did get to do a story of his. I think his historical novel about the life and times of Don John of Austria deserves consideration.

Ana Teresa Torres is a clinical psychologist and must have been well-served by her profession in putting this story together. It is a history of Venezuela and Caracas channeled into a family chronicle narrated by a deceased *grande dame* of the colonial period who must have had something of Brás Cubas about her. Most of the tale is told from beyond the grave, although we do get a bit more of a peep at life after death than we get with Machado.

The first challenge to the translator, as is so often the case, comes with the title. It all has to do with that simple and understandable Spanish word *olvido*. If we take a careful look at the word, however, we find that it has no real English equivalent. It comes from the verb *olvidar*, to forget, so we come up with forgetfulness. No soap. This last term is best applied to the fabled absent-minded professor. *Olvido* has the sense of a state of having been forgotten, for which I am unable to pull out a term in English. The closest would be a manufactured word, forgottenness. This is what the title really means. Psycholinguists must look into this situation in which a common and sensible notion in Spanish cannot be expressed in a like manner in English. The usual inadequate solution was to turn to the term oblivion. The problem here, to my mind, is that oblivion doesn't carry the personal connotation of people's having forgotten someone. A similar problem always arises when the Spanish gives *nada*, nothing, a definitive article, and turns it into a stronger noun, *la nada*. Unamuno uses it all the time and the closest we can come in English is with another awkward word, nothingness. These two examples out of many serve to show the inherent impossibility of translation.

The story here begins with a series of colonial lawsuits regarding the ownership of some land. There is a lot of legal mumbo jumbo that I think I have managed successfully, but *contra* had to be handled with care as it is part of the title. It means against, and as such it leads to many different ways in which it can be used, including legal contests. As the title stands in Spanish, then, it could mean Doña Inés's legal fight to see that her case is not forgotten or just as easily it could be her own personal struggle not to be forgotten herself. Under the inflence of so many cases being bandied about in the press, I thought first of *Doña Inés v. Oblivion*, where the letter would be pronounced as in the Roe v. Wade I hear all the time. This would have limited the scope to the legal and wouldn't have covered Doña Inés's personal struggle against being forgotten. So v. was replaced by vs., which can be applied with equal measure to a lawsuit, an athletic contest, or an election. If the case here were to come before the high court, however, I wonder where Mr. Justice Sharia would stand on the matter.

Doña Inés preserves her honorific in English as is only proper. This form of address has no equivalent in other languages, and attempts to translate the *don* in Don Quixote have failed miserably. There is always a problem with students who think that his name must really be Donald and go along calling him Don. This can be remedied with a simple definite article. *Don* and *doña* are slightly more intimate equivalents of Mr. and Mrs./Miss/Ms., but are used with the first name. The only English equivalents would be Sir and Dame, but for that you have to be knighted. Portuguese has similar terms but while *dona* is the equivalent of *doña*, *dom* is reserved for bishops and kings.

I had to be cautious in the usual places while doing the novel, keeping in mind that Doña Inés was a colonial dame and she was telling the tale, and her descriptions of modern Venezuela are sometimes aptly archaic. The story involves class and racial distinctions and struggles throughout and there had to be differences in the way people talked. Here the translator must denote a character's station by his or her speech but must be wary not to go beyond making the character simply anglophonic. Racial terms and slurs are particularly hard to handle in Latin America because of the welter of distinctions made and the accompanying slurs. The Spanish word *negro*, black, passed into English as a description of race, Negro, which was first capitalized and then done away with. Actually, simply sticking with the translation "black" seems to have worked out. African Venezuelan as in African American would be an absurdity. Now that we have gone back to being what Theodore Roosevelt eschewed as hyphenated Americans, I wonder where that leaves us mules. In my own case I'm not sure how many hyphens will be needed to describe my ethnicity, with even more for my children and grandchildren. Maybe it would be best for me to follow Rick Blaine's answer to Major Strasser in *Casablanca* when asked about his nationality: drunkard, which, as Captain Renault puts it, means a citizen of the world. Getting back to racial slurs and epithets, there is no linguistic equivalent in Spanish for "nigger." It's all done with adjectives and additives. When you hear *negro cabrón* or *negrito* applied to a grown man you should know that you have just heard "nigger." There is little else to do but translate it that way, as I have done.

Darcy Ribeiro

The Brazilian People (*O povo brasileiro*, 1995). Gainesville: University Press of Florida, 2000.

When I was teaching with Charles Wagley at Columbia many were the times Chuck would talk about his experiences and his escapades with the Brazilian anthropologist Darcy Ribeiro, so when I was asked by my former student Elizabeth Lowe to translate his study of the development of the Brazilian people I did not linger in abrogating my oath never to do any more nonfiction. I have no regrets in doing so but I do regret the circumstance that Darcy died before he could see the translation. I was also urged on by the fact that I would be working on a sociological text written by a novelist, as Darcy has two good novels that came before this, *Maíra* and *The Mule*, translated by Elizabeth Lowe, so this study shouldn't be all that bad as far as writing was concerned. Novelist though he might have been, Ribeiro was also a social scientist so it was inevitable that technical terminology should appear in the book. As the majority of these terms are Latinate in origin it was no problem to turn them into English words from the same roots. Others were simply Portuguese translations of Anglo-American jargon, some of which was familiar to me and the rest of which was easily translated back.

As he describes the different types who make up the population of Brazil there is a good deal of local terminology. When translating novels I had no few words for terms like *matuto* and *caipira* which denote rustics, but here I found that such terms are not always general and are apt to describe inhabitants of a particular region and often carry occupational or racial connotations. In many of these cases I found myself preserving the Portuguese word after having defined it with a word or two so that any distinction could be preserved throughout the book. There was a greater variety of material in the book than one might have imagined. Besides the regular text I was also called upon to do quotations from other writers or documents from various periods. In one case I had to do some poetry by Gregório de Matos, the baroque colonial poet from Bahia popularly known as *Boca do Inferno*. It was a nice change and a respite from some of the sociological and economic charts where the terms needed translation.

In this book and in others I have found that there are some items best left in the original. I spoke before of how I handled streets and avenues and we can add to those the Portuguese *praça* and the Spanish *plaza*, which simply mean square. If it carries along a proper name, as in Praça Tiradentes, I leave it as is. Tiradentes Square is a little off base. It would only stand up against the absurdity of Toothpuller Square. When the words are common nouns, however, I do translate them. I doubt that many Americans know what *praça* means and plaza in English suggests other things than squares, more often than not something to do with shopping centers or hostelries. The national drink in Brazil is *cachaça*, cane liquor or raw rum. I am torn here between keeping it or calling it cane liquor, although as more Americans become familiar with things Brazilian they might be familiar with *cachaça* as the main ingredient in a *caipirinha*. In many Spanish cane-growing countries this distillation is called *aguardiente* (burning water), which is the legitimate name for brandy in grape-growing lands. No Pedro Domecq here, so in such cases I must call it cane liquor.

The other troublesome matter is money. I wonder how the Old Testament would come across if we converted shekels into dollars and cents. In both Brazil and Portugal there exists the term *conto*, which transcends any changes in nomenclature or value in matters of currency. It is an unofficial designation and simply means a thousand of whatever the currency happens to be at the moment. I have seen Brazil go from the *cruzeiro* to the *novo cruzeiro* to the *cruzado* and to the *real*. The *conto* covered all these revaluations and renamings. In Portugal we used to have the *escudo* (which GI's in the Azores heard in the plural as skoots and called it thus), which also gave us the *conto* when there were a thousand of them. I wonder if a thousand euros makes the grade. As can be seen, there is enough trouble with the nomenclature without getting into any attempt at a transvaluation into U.S. dollars and cents. Besides, a dollar ain't a dollar anymore.

Like old-time linotypers I learned a lot of Brazilian sociology and anthropology by translating this book and I was fascinated by Darcy's theories as to why Brazilian Portuguese sounds so different from that spoken in the mother country. It was also a good chance to retrieve a lot of information I have in my head and which with the passage of time has become so wedged in that it is often difficult to extract it. Even a non-computing person like me has his problems in downloading.

JOÃO DE MELO

My World Is Not of This Kingdom (*O Meu Mundo Não É Deste Reino*, 1983). Minneapolis: Aliform Publishing, 2003.

I MENTIONED A WHILE BACK that a good source of discovery for works to be translated is books sent me by former students. Quite some time ago I received a novel from a student I had known as April Monteiro but who over the years had become Professor Adelaide Baptista and was teaching American studies at the University of the Azores. I glanced through the book, saw the same dinosaur-egg simile I had seen in *One Hundred Years of Solitude*, and right off I knew that I was on to something. I set about reading the novel at once and found that I was getting close to Macondo. But let me say here and now that Rozário is no more Macondo than Macondo is Lagado or Laputa. They are all one and the same simultaneously. Much talk has been made about Everyman, but there has been little mention of Everytown. Its embodiments have been legion, from Winesburg, Ohio, to Yoknapatawpha County. Therefore, I get annoyed with myopic reviewers who, like me, spot the dinosaur eggs, but then go on railing about how Melo is nothing but an imitator of García Márquez. Are these the fruits of intertextuality, whatever that is? I have translated both authors and I am someone who was trained to spot phony intelligence and I can aver that there is no imitation here, only that universal coincidence that accompanies the human condition. As a matter of fact, since the culture of the Azores is a bit older than that of Colombia, Achadinha and Rozário antedate Macondo. Let us leave the matter there and leave the nits at rest.

In the translation business, if one wants either recompense or recognition it is more judicious to await the call. This I learned particularly well with *My World*. As I read the book I kept saying to myself, "I've got to do this, it's asking me to translate it." So I went about translating the novel completely on my own. Adelaide had given me João's address in Lisbon and I got in touch with him to help me along with any difficulties. When the book came out at long last Katherine Vaz and Onésimo Almeida had lent good hands in nailing down some of the Azoreanisms.

I'm rather far removed from the world of merchants and the peddling of their wares, so I never got very far in my attempts to find a publisher. Julie Popkin, the agent, did her best, but nothing came of it until some years later it fell into the hands of another old student of mine, Jay Miskowiec, who had set up a publishing house in Minneapolis. Talk about old boy/girl networks! Out of all this I'm left with some advice for translators: if you're not the go-getter type, you'd best be satisfied with the fact that anything unassigned you might be doing will have to be a labor of love and will provide naught but the great satisfaction of having done it.

João de Melo's prose is quite fluid in what we could call its eloquence, so I let myself be carried along by it as usual. Some of his names have meaning in Portuguese but come close enough to the English version for me to leave them as they were: Father Governo, Cadete the Healer, and some few others. The mayor of Achadinha had been given the nickname of

Goraz, elephant fish. After a quick definition of the name I left it that way because of the important virtue of its sound as applied to the despicable character who bore it. I made a strong effort to follow the typographical peculiarities João used in parts of the novel, capitalizing certain portions and such, and I'm glad that the typesetter had no trouble in following along, so I can forgive him for Hispanizing the surname Mendonça into Mendoça. I'm quite pleased with the edition Jay has brought out and I hope that any number of deserving and overlooked works from Latin America and the Iberian Peninsula will find their way to him.

I only met João once, when he and Adelaide were passing through New York and dropped by. I was pleased to discover that he was a good friend of my other Portuguese novelist, António Lobo Antunes. Putting their books side by side one can see that genius has no shape of its own but takes on that of whom it has endowed with its presence. I must never offend this unique grace with any hint in my translations that I am lurking behind the originators. Melo has other novels, among them a fine chronicle of emigration from the Azores, *Gente Feliz com Lágrimas*, with a beautifully ambivalent title that can be translated either as "Happy People with Tears" or "People Happy with Tears." I hope that someone will pick up on this good tale.

JESÚS ZÁRATE

Jail (*La cárcel*, 1972). Minneapolis: Aliform Publishing, 2003.

ZÁRATE'S SON NÉSTOR, WHO WAS living in New York at the time, came to me with the proposal that I do his father's prize-winning novel *La cárcel* and that he would seek a publisher afterwards. A quick perusal showed me that I had something good and the arrangement fit in with my plans, so I went to work. As it turned out, this book, too, came to be published by Jay Miskowiec's Aliform Publishing. I can only say that I hope his future publications will be in the same category as the two I did for him. Jesús Zárate, from Colombia, was at work before his better-known compatriot García Márquez, but he had been left out of the international acclaim that landed on his countryman and others of that generation. This novel did win the coveted Planeta Prize in Spain. Why are prizes always called "coveted," as if the contenders were a greedy bunch rubbing their hands in conspiratorial or lascivious anticipation? There is a story here, which might bear out something of what I just said. Jesús Zarate had died between his submission and the awarding of the prize, which is supposed to go to a living author. A final verdict came down allowing that since the author had been alive when the book was chosen, he could be awarded the prize posthumously. There was a great flurry among the runners-up, all of which made me think of Doña Inés or whether Brás Cubas's memoirs would have been eligible, but all has thankfully been capped with the translation of the novel and the publication of a new edition in Spanish.

This book is somewhat different from what one might expect in that it's a jailhouse diary kept by one of four cellmates and it tells of their activities and talk during the day specified for each entry. The narrator is one Antonio Castán, who has shortened his name to Antón, for seemingly strange but ultimately natural reasons. He is the one who is keeping the diary. The others are David, who is called a writer but we find out that what he had written were forged checks; Braulio, a bigamist house painter; and the fascinating Mister Alba, a man of many parts. Although it is Antón who is reporting all the dialogues and conversations, they manage to maintain a touch of the personalities involved and I had to make sure that the voices were not homogeneous. The translator must always listen to the characters' voices as they come over into English and not his or her voice as they are being translated. I didn't seem to have had much trouble with this, although I did have to be careful with Mister Alba. He had assumed the English honorific while working in the Canal Zone in Panama. It isn't a translation of *señor* but is *mister* in the original. There was no way I could make sure that this was understood except through some unwanted explanatory intrusion, which I wouldn't have. I think I may have helped to put this across by maintaining the full spelling of the word instead of using *Mr.*

The novel is full of ambiguities, ambivalences, and what we might even call mysteries. Antón claims innocence, which is not unusual for prisoners, and that he was framed for a murder, which leads up to his committing another murder in prison, thus justifying his presence there. I had to be careful as

I went through the book not to destroy any of the nuances and to leave all the ambiguities intact for the readers to figure out. As usual, each reader will be reading a different book, and in this case might well be pondering a different ending. Once again we have fiction within the fiction as Mister Alba tells his varying and various tales with no evidence at hand as to whether he is telling the truth or not, much in the manner of Borges. If truth really is beauty then it is easy for eloquence to masquerade as such and thus get away with a lie. I have found this to be the case when I've tried to pawn off *Pas de lieu Rhône que nous* as a particularly arcane line from Verlaine or Valéry while it is naught but an ancient Abenaki adage.

JORGE FRANCO

Rosario Tijeras (*Rosario Tijeras*, 1999). New York: Seven Stories Press, 2004.

THIS IS THE LATEST BOOK I have translated to have appeared in print. Others await a publisher and I hope that like *My World* they will find one eventually. When I first got *Rosario Tijeras* I wondered if I would be up to and adequate for the translation of a book from the new generation. Aspects and outlooks have both changed over my years and I still feel quite anchored in my own time, which is long gone. There are many moments when I feel like a time traveler and, by God, that I am, even if the journey has been so gradual that I haven't noticed such as I've headed along. After I got into the book I found that I wasn't all that distant from the story. Maybe it's because it's a Latin American tale and I've been a traveler there, too, although more in space than in time. Even so I'm saddened by changes in places I've been. Strange it is that in New York I miss the time of the Third Avenue El while in Rio I miss the time when there was no Metrô. What I found in Jorge Franco's novel was that globalization has extended itself to criminal activities as well. This is a book about the demi-monde of Medellín, Colombia, what we used to call the un-derworld, and it's all so tellingly similar to our Mafia here. A movie of the novel is under way and Franco is involved in it since cinema is his other calling. What I see would be a rather old-fashioned George Raft movie if the shooting script follows the book, because I didn't find much violence of the explosive fire-and-smoke type we have in current films out of Hollywood.

The title, as is so often the case, provided me with the first problem. Rosario Tijeras is a killer, what we used to call a gun moll in the old Chicago days of Edward G. Robinson's Rico. She comes from the tough hillside slums of Medellín, a city famous now not for its coffee but for its drug cartel and the violent concomitant activities thereof. Tijeras is not her surname but a nickname meaning scissors or shears, given her because of her early deed in using her mother's sewing instrument to geld the man who had raped her as a young girl. Since the epithet is used throughout the book as well as in the title, as though it were her surname, I stayed with it, adding a one- or two-word definition the first time around. I've used this technique before and have found that it can be managed as long as it's done briefly and subtly without interfering with the flow of the text.

I was spared a great deal of concern by the fact that Jorge's use of language is crisp and direct. There's not too much of the outlandish slang we find so much in current American movies and books, the kind of stuff that will quickly follow "23 skidoo" into the realm of the cutesy archaic. Also, the stately Castilian tongue still smacks of Cid Rodrigo Díaz even when it is used for the lowest and earthiest of activities and thus can be translated into rather straightforward English. One local term did give trouble, however. It is *parcero* and it's what Rosario calls Antonio, the narrator, on so many occasions. I fooled around with a lot of terms like "old chum" and "old buddy," none of which really hit the mark. The editors finally went with "old friend." I would have preferred something a little jazzier like "buddy boy," which I think is closer in time if not in place, but I saw no reason to cause any great stir over it. After all, a translation also belongs to the editors since it is a collective enterprise, starting with the author and his or her original version.

I only met Jorge on the occasion of a couple of joint readings in New York and I was struck by his youthful look, leading me once more to wonder if a difference in age has any effect on the translation of a contemporary work and if it might not be comparable to the fantasy of Homer's translating Chapman. I think not. In fact it might well be that a set of older eyes might see things in a more universal light and thus extract the permanence of the text better. Had I been a different age I might have used that horrid verb "to universalize" above and not thought of it, Joyce-wise, as universal eyes. The caution of age does save one from many pitfalls.

This book is my latest published translation, but there are a couple of manuscripts waiting in the wings.

Volodia Teitelboim

Internal War (*La guerra interna*, 1979). Awaiting a publisher.

QUITE SOME YEARS BACK I was called by the Chilean painter
Gastón Orellana, who wanted to discuss the translation of a
novel about the coup against the government of Chile by Au-
gusto Pinochet. I met with him and Volodia's son Claudio, at
the time a professor of physics in Texas. Since they would un-
derwrite the translation I was glad to do my bit in exposing
the takeover by the usurper and the butchery of his cohort of
garrison soldiers, so valiant in going up against the unarmed.
The author, who had been head of the Communist Party, had
fortunately escaped capture and was in Madrid, from where he
would send me copies of a new review he founded called
Araucaria de Chile. As a leading Communist he most certainly
would have been done in, partly in recompense for the fact
that Pinochet and his chocolate soldiers were constrained
from harming the dying Pablo Neruda, a national monument,
much as their confreres the gorillas in Brazil had to leave Jorge
Amado alone. This novel is not magic realism, it is magic
surrealism. The torturers of the regime had been given names
by their victims, who drew them from characters in horror
movies. According to this story Dracula and others had been
sent for and recruited from Hollywood to come down and do

their dirty work. They were nicknames no longer; they were the real thing. Having grown up with those fine old movies I had the necessary depth of imagination to envision these characters and see them go about plying their trade. Glimpses of Nazi leftovers in Italy like the Ardeatine Caves had also provided me with a picture of what events in Chile were like.

Another aspect of the fantastic or magical was the presence of Neruda's ghost, who would visit, advise, and console a young woman who was his goddaughter as she went about in search of her missing husband or for news of him at least. In this part there are pictures of the different places where prisoners were being held for torture and extermination as they were "disappeared." It took the gorillas in Chile, Argentina, and Brazil to make that verb transitive. Since Volodia had been a close friend of Neruda's and subsequently wrote a biography of the poet, what Neruda's spirit had to say had the ring of reality to it.

As years went by I kept waiting for news of the publication of the translation, but it wasn't to be. This, perhaps, is another example of the many vicissitudes of it all. Even when a book has been translated before being offered to a publisher there's no greater possibility of its being done than if it had only been suggested. Here we have something that's a good tale and also sheds some additional light on the human cost of Chile's economic boom. I like to hope that there was no censorship at work, but one never knows. Things like that can turn out to be just as surreal as this very novel.

JOSÉ SARNEY

Master of the Sea (*O Dono do Mar,* 1995). Awaiting a publisher.
Saraminda (*Saraminda,* 2000). Awaiting a publisher.

YEARS BACK CLEM AND I were invited to a State Department
luncheon in honor of President Sarney of Brazil who was in
Washington on a state visit. In the receiving line I introduced
myself as Jorge Amado's translator and the president commented that they were good friends now, meaning that past
political differences had been healed. This made sense later
when I discovered that Sarney was also a writer and member
of the Brazilian Academy of Letters. Some time later I had occasion to meet him again when he spoke on the Portuguese
language at the Camões Institute at Columbia, then under the
tutelage of Kenneth Maxwell. At that meeting I spoke to him
about the work I was doing on Padre Antônio Vieira, which
interested him as a native and former governor of the state of
Maranhão in northeastern Brazil, where Vieira had done some
of his most active missionary work. Then, more recently, I was
contacted by Sarney's aide to see if I would be interested in
translating one of his novels. I accepted and got to work. A
while later Sarney came to New York and we had lunch together and had a chance to talk about the work I was doing
and to clear up any problems that might have shown up in it.

The novel shows once more that what people call magic realism is still extant in Latin America from the way the book deals with the life of the fishermen of coastal Maranhão. The customs and manners of the place can be seen as stark realism evolves into legends, and in the novel there are scenes of local magic along with phantoms from the past who take on physical form. The Maranhão coast has a history of maritime disasters. One of Brazil's best-known early poets, Gonçalves Dias, died in a shipwreck there as he returned from Lisbon. The title of the novel is *O Dono do Mar*, literally the owner of the sea. I found this a bit drab and opted for another possible meaning, *Master of the Sea*, which does give a hint of ownership, or at least domination, and can be related to the title *mestre*, the master of a vessel, preserving the maritime feeling.

I had the first chapter published in a literary review for an issue dedicated to translated works, where it was edited a bit beyond where I would have taken it. So far I've heard nothing about publication of the novel. I haven't been very good at being an agent myself, partly because of a natural disinclination to go about bearding people, but more likely from the fact that in such matters I an inherently lazy. I like to write or even hold forth before a class, but I do have a great aversion to matters calling for a certain push.

At the moment I am working on Sarney's second novel, *Saraminda*, which is quite different from the first and deals with the gold rush in the region where Brazil and French Guiana touch, an area that has been in dispute between the two countries. Today it is part of the new Brazilian state of Amapá, of which José Sarney is now senator and, by extension, president of the Brazilian senate. There are those who say that he has more power now than when he was president of Brazil.

While *Master of the Sea* kept me working as I sought out equivalents for piscatorial and maritime terms, now I have to be on the alert for those dealing with gold prospecting and gathering. Saraminda is the name of a Créole girl from French Guiana. She has been brought to the gold fields by a Brazilian prospector who has a sizable claim worked by many hands. Saraminda has magical qualities, which relate this novel to the earlier one, and in such matters I must be especially careful because some of these terms are deceptively ordinary. The French language also appears, as the scene of a great deal of the action is Cayenne. I leave the French intact because that is how Brazilians have seen it in the original. This is the way in which I have always handled such matters in the past where a third language was involved.

Since I haven't finished the translation I can't say how the story comes out, but from the way it is told, back and forth in flashbacks, I have some inklings. All I can hope for is that I won't have to go back and make too many changes when I'm through. I also hope that this novel will be picked up along with its predecessor when it's done. They both deserve the attention of English-speaking readers, who will be quite well rewarded.

THE PLAYS

René Marqués, *Death Shall Not Enter the Palace* (*La muerte no entrará en palacio*). Puerto Rican Traveling Theatre, 1981.

Jaime Carrero, *Betances* (*Betances*). Puerto Rican Traveling Theatre, 1981.

José Ruibal, *The Man and the Fly* (*El hombre y la mosca*). Puerto Rican Traveling Theatre, 1981.

Fernando Arrabal, *Inquisition* (*Inquisición*). Puerto Rican Traveling Theatre, 1983.

Pedro Calderón de la Barca, *David's Crown* (*Los cabellos de Absalón*). Tony Randall Repertory Company (awaiting production).

I'VE HAD SOME SCANT experience in doing plays, the greatest number for Miriam Colón and her vibrant Puerto Rican Traveling Theatre, which, when I was doing plays for her, had stopped traveling a bit and had settled down in a wonderfully renovated former firehouse in the Fifties, west of the regular theater district. Two of the plays dealt with Puerto Rican political history and two were by Spanish authors. I've forgotten a great deal about them but I did attend the performances and I was pleased to hear my words as they made sense coming out of the Spanish.

Clem and I were lucky to have attended a preliminary

reading of *The Man and the Fly* at Miriam's home, where José Ferrer and Raúl Juliá took a crack at reading the two-man play. I was singularly happy to hear my words coming out of their mouths and I enjoyed the feeling much more than I do when I reread a translation of mine that has appeared in print, even when I approve of it. Unfortunately they were unable to do the play and Rip Torn played the lead. Pepé Ruibal was there and we enjoyed his company and his talk. When he returned to Madrid he sent us one of his artist sister's paintings which hangs next to the one given me by Gastón Orellana when I was working on Volodia Teitelboim's book. I only have vague recollections of Arrabal's play, although I did also see it performed.

Tony Randall had seen Calderón's play about David and Absalom performed in Hebrew in Israel. He said he couldn't understand all the words but he did understand the play and he wanted it done for his repertory group, which was then in formation. I did the play and he approved the translation, but evidently his company was having the usual difficulties and the play was never performed. I've taught Calderón and I was familiar with his baroque cadences, although I found this play to be quite a bit more straightforward than *Life Is a Dream*. I had also read extensively in his Elizabethan contemporaries and I knew how they sounded. I had to be wary of making him too Shakespearean on the one hand but also seeing to it that he didn't sound like Arthur Miller on the other. Here again I let nature, my nature, take its course, seeking the logical and avoiding the outlandish, which can be difficult when dealing with Calderón, although not all that much with this play.

With plays I had to think about production and not reading. Actors must of needs "project," as they say, quite unlike the reading of dialogue or a monologue in a novel. The words used, therefore, have to be of the kind that can carry into the balcony. I had to keep in mind that I, like Calderón, was writing for full-throated people and not for Herbert Marshall, who always seems to be saying "waffle, waffle." These are the only plays I've done and I enjoyed seeing them acted out, quite a different experience from a silent reading. There is always the actor, who adds his or her voice to that of the author and that of the translator. I heard things I didn't know were there, much as would be the experience of hearing someone reading the text of a novel aloud. Hearing the words was a good lesson for any future dialogue I might have to translate in fiction.

PART THREE

BY WAY OF A VERDICT

How Say You?

ALL HAS NOW BEEN SHOWN and we come to the moment of truth, the *vere dictum*, what is truly said. To my ear this sounds quite like something translation itself might be aspiring to say in an attempt to get us off the hook. Here we are, using a translation from Latin in a specious defense of translation. That old doubting Latinophonic Pilate might not have accepted the argument that translation is but another version of the truth. Then again, in Spain *la hora de la verdad* means killing the bull, which can also mean in popular parlance to stop going on about this. In order to render a verdict we need a jury, but who is it to be? Throughout my disquisition I have savaged just about everyone eligible. It has been a *voir dire* that would have produced a hanged jury rather than a hung one. So I am left, as the cliché goes, to be both judge and jury. Here my ambivalent and ambiguous nature makes a decision difficult, approaching the impossible, just as translation, in reverse, can only approach the possible and never get there. I think that Kaspar Gutman would have been pleased with me, saying to Sam Spade, "I like a man who can go in either direction or none at all. You can't trust a man who's sure of himself. He's hard and brittle and runs the risk of falling apart on you."

All of this has been borne out by my ultimate dissatisfaction with any translation I have done, even the most praiseworthy. This would suggest, then, that there has been some kind of treason afoot. As judge, therefore, I must render what is called a Scots verdict: not proven. We translators will not be shot at cock's crow, but neither shall we walk about free of our own doubts that we may have somehow done something treasonable in our work. As for this particular piece of work,

> There will be no *sine die*
> until night devours day
> and the FIN is dorsal.